# Cracking the Cybersecurity Job Interview

## MARIA BRYGHT

Copyright © 2024 Maria Bryght

# DEDICATION

To the pioneers and protectors of the digital frontier,

This book is dedicated to the guardians of cyberspace—the tireless defenders, innovative problem solvers, and visionary thinkers who navigate the intricate maze of our digital world. With gratitude, we recognize your unwavering commitment to safeguarding our virtual landscapes, ensuring the security of our data, and preserving the integrity of our online communities.

May this work serve as a testament to your resilience, a celebration of your achievements, and a beacon for future cybersecurity professionals. In these pages, we explore the challenges you face and the victories you secure, inspired by your dedication to a safer digital tomorrow.

# CONTENTS

# ACKNOWLEDGEMENTS

First and foremost, my gratitude goes to the myriad cybersecurity professionals I've had the honor of interacting with. Their willingness to share knowledge, challenge conventional wisdom, and push the boundaries of what is possible in digital defense has been nothing short of inspirational. To you, the experts in the trenches of cyber warfare, ethical hacking, digital forensics, and information security management, thank you for your invaluable contributions and for illuminating the path forward.

Lastly, to my family and friends: your unwavering support, understanding, and encouragement have been my anchor throughout this process. The sacrifices made and the belief you have shown in me and this project have been the source of my strength and resilience.

# INTRODUCTION

Welcome to your comprehensive guide to navigating the challenging and competitive landscape of cybersecurity employment. In today's digital age, where the importance of protecting data and information systems has never been more critical, the field of cybersecurity has emerged as a dynamic and rewarding career path. However, with high demand comes high standards, and securing a position in this sector requires more than just technical acumen; it requires preparation, strategy, and insight into what employers are truly seeking.

This book is designed for anyone aspiring to break into the cybersecurity industry, whether you're a recent graduate, a professional transitioning from another field, or an experienced practitioner aiming for a higher-level position. We understand that the job interview can often be the most daunting part of the job search process. It is the stage where theory meets practice, where skills are tested, and where first impressions can make or break your chances of securing your desired role.

This is not just another interview tips book. It is a deep dive into the heart of the cybersecurity job market, offering you a clear understanding of what employers are looking for, the various roles available within the field, and the specific skills and knowledge you need to demonstrate. We cover everything from crafting your resume to match the cybersecurity industry's expectations, to navigating technical interviews, to handling behavioral questions with confidence.

Each chapter in this book is structured to guide you through different components of the cybersecurity job interview process, with real-world scenarios, example questions and answers, insider tips from hiring managers, and practical advice on how to present your experience and skills in the best light. We'll also explore the latest trends in cybersecurity, including the impact of emerging technologies and how they are shaping the skills requirements of the industry.

Our goal is to not only help you pass the cybersecurity job interview but to do so with a level of preparedness and confidence that sets you apart from other candidates. Whether your dream is to become a Cybersecurity Analyst, a Penetration Tester, a Security Architect, or any other role within this diverse field, this book is your roadmap to achieving that dream.

Embark on this journey with us, as we help you navigate the path to not just passing the cybersecurity job interview, but excelling in it. Your future in cybersecurity starts here.

Delving into cybersecurity job interviews can be seen through a lens quite similar to conducting a penetration test on a network. Just as in penetration testing, where one must first understand and survey the network landscape, identify potential vulnerabilities, and then proceed to exploit these findings, cracking the code of cybersecurity job interviews demands a similar strategic approach. It's about dissecting the hiring process, recognizing what drives recruiters, and effectively "penetrating" the interview stages.

In your journey, you will typically encounter five distinct phases of the interview process: Initial screening with a recruiter, interview with the hiring manager, conversations with potential colleagues (peer interview), a practical or theoretical task (assignment interview) and a final hurdle: meeting with a C-level person.

While on the surface, they may all appear to be variations of the same process, each stage is uniquely tailored, focusing on distinct aspects depending on the interviewer's role and the point in the process you've reached. As we delve deeper, you'll come to see how the dynamics of your interaction with a hiring manager will significantly diverge from those in your meeting with a C-level person.

Before diving into the main method, let's start with the **basic general questions**, needed to form a solid structure for you to start from.

# THE BASICS

## What to expect from each stage

Following your application submission, if your profile piques their interest, expect a callback from an HR representative or a recruiter. This initial touchpoint typically unfolds as a phone interview lasting between 15 to 30 minutes. During this conversation, the recruiter is chiefly seeking to ascertain three aspects: firstly, the alignment of your skills and background with the job requirements; secondly, your ability to communicate clearly and efficiently; and thirdly, your enthusiasm and vigor for the position. Your presentation in this phone interview is crucial, given the absence of visual cues. Hence, it's vital to exude positivity and articulate your responses concisely.

Should you progress beyond this preliminary stage, the subsequent phase generally involves a face-to-face encounter with the hiring manager. This meeting demands that you come prepared with pertinent anecdotes from your career, explicitly tying them to the job at hand. Ultimately, your compatibility with the organization's culture and your rapport with the interviewer will significantly influence the offer decision. Therefore, aim to genuinely connect during this interaction. If you find yourself addressing multiple interviewers, ensure to engage with each person present, giving special attention even to those who might be more reserved.

The interview journey often culminates with a discussion with a senior executive, such as a director. This final round shifts focus away from your technical prowess—already established in earlier rounds—towards a deeper exploration of your personal fit within the company culture. Expect a more informal dialogue rather than a structured question-and-answer session. However, staying prepared with relevant experiences is still advisable, as your job-related competencies might be revisited. This concluding interview is your opportunity to solidify that crucial connection with the executive, leaving them assured that you are indeed the right choice for the role.

## Body language

Navigating body language during interviews is crucial for creating a comfortable atmosphere for both you and the interviewer. It's natural to experience nerves before an interview, but it's important to manage your internal state because it inevitably influences your external presentation. To mitigate this, consider adopting the mindset of a consultant rather than a job seeker. A consultant enters discussions aware of their worth and the benefits they can provide, instilling a sense of confidence and ease in their demeanor.

Another strategy is to mirror the interviewer's body language. If they lean forward, do the same to demonstrate engagement. Should they share a light-hearted moment, join in with laughter. This mirroring technique fosters a connection and keeps both parties actively involved in the conversation.

Lastly, maintaining presence is essential. It's easy to get lost in your thoughts, worrying about the interviewer's perception. However, grounding yourself, such as by focusing on the sensation of your feet against the floor, can bring your attention back to the moment. Active listening not only improves the quality of your responses but also ensures you're fully engaged in the dialogue.

By focusing on these three aspects—projecting ease, mirroring body language, and staying present—you can enhance your non-verbal communication and make a positive impact in your interviews.

### How to properly research the company

Firstly, dive deep into the company's official website. Beyond the "About Us" section, seek out information pertinent to the position you're applying for. If you're in finance and the company is publicly traded, explore the investor relations page for financial reports and data. Secondly, utilize Google News to stay updated with the latest developments or press statements concerning the company. Highlighting your knowledge about recent events, such as acquisitions, and how you can contribute with your skills can be beneficial.

Thirdly, leverage LinkedIn to connect with current or former employees of the company. Arrange a brief chat over coffee or a call to gain valuable insights and advice for your interview. Additionally, familiarize yourself with the profiles of the individuals who will be interviewing you, understanding their backgrounds to make the conversation smoother.

Fourthly, review the company's presence on social media platforms like Twitter, Instagram, and Facebook. These platforms can provide insights into the company's culture, priorities, and the broader trends they are engaged with.

In summary, thorough research involves reviewing the company's website, staying informed with Google News, networking on LinkedIn, and analyzing social media content. This approach will equip you with a comprehensive understanding of the company's ethos, activities, and how you can align your contributions.

### How to dress for the interview

Here are four key strategies to impress the moment you enter the interview room. First, do your homework, not guesswork. Understand their company culture - is it formal or more laid back? Examine their website and social media for clues. Peek at group photos or employees' LinkedIn recommendations. If their vibe is casual, elevate your attire slightly to demonstrate your commitment to the role, even if the interviewer opts for a more relaxed look. Second, ensure your clothing fits well. If you've recently lost weight, update your wardrobe to match your new size, avoiding any mishaps or ill-fitting garments that detract from your professionalism.

Third, stay true to your style. This isn't the occasion for a radical wardrobe experiment that might leave you feeling awkward. Opt for outfits that boost your self-assurance, steering clear of any fashion choices that don't reflect your true self, such as an out-of-character vest suggested by a friend. Lastly, keep it understated. Shy away from excessive perfume, too much jewelry, or overly bold colors that might dominate the conversation. Your aim is for your attire to be noted for its appropriateness, not as a distracting statement. Your appearance should confidently whisper, "I'm the right choice for this position."

### Post interview

The silence following an interview can unsettle even the most self-assured candidates, creating unwelcome stress. To navigate this effectively, consider employing a straightforward follow-up approach that maintains your composure and exudes confidence. Initially, it's wise to inquire about the next steps and the expected timeline before departing the interview. Often, interviewers may indicate a timeline, such as concluding initial interviews by the following week. Knowing this helps you maintain peace of mind until the specified time lapses.

If there's no word by the indicated time, or if you didn't establish a timeframe during the interview, sending a polite follow-up email after a week is advisable. Frame your message positively, perhaps mentioning your enthusiasm about a specific topic discussed, like their expansion strategy, and offer to provide any further details they might need. Delays in the hiring process are common due to various reasons, such as internal discussions or workload surges. A gentle yet assertive email can prompt progress.

Should there be no reply, reaching out to a company insider for insights can be beneficial. While it may not expedite the process, understanding the situation can ease your mind. If continued silence persists for an additional week or two, consider sending another follow-up before moving on. Bombarding the hiring team with messages can be counterproductive and potentially detrimental to your application. Maintain a positive outlook, focus on what you can influence, and stay composed throughout the process.

### Tell me about yourself

This prompt might seem puzzling. Is it truly a question? Not in the traditional sense, yet it's a staple of job interviews, often serving as the opening volley. Far from being a query to dread, this is your golden chance to start the interview on a high note. Here are three essential tips to master your introduction.

Firstly, embrace the 'SHE' strategy: be Succinct, Honest, and Engaging. This isn't the moment for a lengthy chronicle of your entire career. Avoid reciting your CV verbatim. Interviewers seek a concise demonstration of your suitability for the position and your ability to handle open-ended questions. And that's easier than it sounds, which leads us to the second tip.

Utilize the job listing as your guide. Ahead of the interview, review the job description, noting key skills and requirements that align with your expertise. Whether it's problem-solving prowess, ease in public speaking, or excellence in customer service, identify these areas. Then, think about how you can present your narrative in a way that highlights these strengths, while also infusing your response with personality and relatable anecdotes. For instance, you might share how a volunteer project sparked your passion for non-profit work, or recount fond memories of helping out at your grandparents' bed and breakfast, illustrating your love for hospitality. The key is to connect your personal story to the job in a clear, authentic manner.

### What is your greatest strength?

Approaching this question might seem straightforward, yet it's quite the opposite. It's crucial not to appear overconfident or boastful. Instead, aim for a tone of humility, and there are strategies to ensure your response is impactful. First off, select experiences that directly relate to the role you're applying for. For instance, if you're seeking a position in sales, share an instance where your solution directly addressed a customer's need. Secondly, detail matters. Describe how solving that issue contributed to achieving a significant portion of your yearly goals.

In narrating your experiences, blend both soft and technical skills. For example, if effective communication is your forte, recount a situation where this skill facilitated a meaningful discussion with a higher-up. Or, if you've spearheaded a tech initiative, illustrate how a meticulously crafted project plan led to its successful execution. As someone responsible for hiring, such stories reassure me of your potential to enhance the team's productivity. It's important to demonstrate that you're a collaborative individual who will positively impact the team dynamic.

### What is your biggest weakness?

Reflecting on this question brings several key points to the forefront. Firstly, embracing humility and authenticity is crucial. Share a genuine story that highlights your self-awareness and willingness to acknowledge imperfections. This honesty fosters trust, which is essential for the position you're seeking. Secondly, avoid pointing out a flaw that could directly undermine your ability to fulfill the job requirements. Opt for a weakness that's less central to the job's core competencies. For instance, if you're aiming for a project management position, you might discuss a challenge with creativity rather than a critical operational skill.

Thirdly, it's beneficial to demonstrate a proactive approach to overcoming your weaknesses. If you find it difficult to keep track of product specifics and you use your phone or a notebook to manage this, sharing this strategy indicates your dedication to improvement and problem-solving.

In summary, there are three strategic moves to consider: remain genuine and humble, choose a non-essential weakness, and showcase your commitment to self-improvement with a concrete plan of action.

**Why should be hire you?**

This question can indeed be daunting, prompting you to consider various outcomes to ensure success. I believe adopting a three-part strategy can significantly aid in crafting an effective response. Firstly, establish your eligibility for the role. Choose three or four aspects of your background that clearly demonstrate your suitability and make it easy for the interviewer(s) to see you in the role.

Next, illustrate your potential impact within the position. Highlight unique achievements or abilities that set you apart from others. Thirdly, beyond qualifications, emphasize your compatibility with the company culture. Discuss your alignment with their mission, values, and operational style, showing why you'd seamlessly integrate into their environment.

A crucial, often overlooked aspect is the manner of your communication. Conveying your achievements and answers with genuineness allows interviewers to genuinely connect with you, evaluating not just your skills but your fit within the team dynamic. Remember, presenting the best, most authentic version of yourself is key.

**Why do you want to work with us?**

Here are three effective tactics to consider. Firstly, prioritize the company's interests. Tempting as it may be to highlight personal benefits like tuition reimbursement programs, focus instead on the employer's perspective. An impactful response demonstrates your awareness of the company's goals and how you can add value to their team. Remember, businesses are primarily focused on profitability, growth, and mission fulfillment. They're keen to understand how you fit into these objectives. This approach sets you apart, as surprisingly few candidates tackle this angle effectively, presenting a prime opportunity for you to stand out.

After establishing how you align with the company's needs, you can then subtly introduce your personal motivations in a manner that underscores your contributions. For example, if you possess expertise in accounting and are applying to a finance position within a nonprofit focused on animal welfare, you might express how the role marries your professional acumen with your love for animals.

Lastly, authenticity goes a long way. Being sincere in your responses makes a lasting impression. I recall advising a client who aspired to be a zoo event manager. Having grown up adjacent to the zoo she applied to, she shared cherished memories of peacocks wandering into her yard. Her desire to create similarly joyful experiences for others at the zoo was a compelling and heartfelt reason for wanting the job. Aim for that level of personal connection in your response.

### What would your co-workers say about you?

From an early age, many of us are taught the virtue of humility, making it challenging to openly celebrate our achievements. Consequently, when an interview question nudges us towards self-promotion, it can feel somewhat awkward. Interviewers are aware of this discomfort, which is why they might frame the question as, "What would your coworkers say about you?" This indirect approach encourages you to highlight your strengths without feeling boastful. To tackle this question effectively, consider these three strategies.

Firstly, align your response with the job description and your understanding of the role. The aim here isn't to boast about unrelated skills, such as your prowess in office sports, but to demonstrate how you fit the specific requirements of the position. For example, if the role demands a proficient problem-solver, you might mention being dubbed as 'Mr. Fix-It' by your colleagues due to your knack for addressing complex issues.

Secondly, sift through your LinkedIn endorsements and performance appraisals prior to the interview. Often, the feedback you've already received contains valuable insights that can serve as the basis for your answer. Highlighting a specific commendation from LinkedIn can also direct interviewers to verify and read more about your contributions.

Lastly, substantiate your claims with concrete examples. If you believe your colleagues would praise your creativity, opt for sharing a specific incident where your innovative thinking directly contributed to a project's success, ensuring it's relevant to the responsibilities of the job you're applying for.

This question is a golden chance to present your exceptional qualities in a manner that feels genuine rather than like you're merely bragging. Embrace this opportunity to showcase your value.

### Why do you want to leave your current position?

When faced with this query, my guidance is straightforward. First and foremost, maintain a positive tone. Avoid the pitfall of speaking negatively about your present position, company, or supervisor. Secondly, frame your response to emphasize the aspirations and objectives you have for your forthcoming role. Lastly, ensure your aspirations align with the attributes and responsibilities of the job you're currently interviewing for. This approach helps you articulate your career movement in a constructive and forward-looking manner.

### Can you explain this gap on your resume?

Addressing gaps in your resume can feel daunting; I've yet to encounter a job seeker who brushes off concerns about employment breaks as trivial. It's common to worry about the perception of such gaps, despite having legitimate reasons for them. The encouraging part is, if you've been called for an interview, the gap hasn't disqualified you, but be prepared to discuss it. Here's how:

Firstly, prioritize honesty. A straightforward explanation is key— embellishment is unnecessary and risks future complications. If your position was eliminated due to restructuring, state it plainly.

Secondly, present your situation with confidence and without regret. Showing embarrassment or unease about time taken off can negatively influence the interviewer's perception. It's similar to reacting to a child's fall: your reaction influences theirs. A calm and assured explanation helps the interviewer feel more comfortable with your employment history.

Lastly, highlight the positives from your gap period. Whether it was due to a layoff, family commitments, or a dismissal, focus on the beneficial outcomes and the skills you developed during this time. Demonstrating how these experiences have equipped you with valuable skills for the job can turn a potential negative into a compelling part of your candidacy.

### What are your salary expectations?

Discussing salary expectations is a common yet crucial part of job interviews. First, avoid stating a precise salary figure right off the bat. It's more strategic to suggest a salary range. Offering too low a figure might undermine your value, whereas a too-high figure could inadvertently exclude you from consideration. Hence, the importance of balance.

Second, engage in thorough market research to inform the salary range you propose. Mention that your expectations are based on comprehensive market analysis, which helps set a benchmark for compensation discussions.

Regarding finding reliable salary data, there are various online resources available. Online Salary Tools are particularly useful, leveraging vast data to offer insights on a wide array of positions, covering over a thousand job titles. This can serve as a solid foundation for your salary discussions.

Lastly, don't overlook the potential of negotiating signing bonuses. This can be an effective method to close any gaps in salary negotiations.

By adhering to these three recommendations, you'll be better equipped to handle conversations about salary expectations with confidence.

### What do you like to do outside of work?

When an interviewer inquires about your interests outside of work, they're seeking insight into your personality and how you might fit into the company's culture. Your goal is to leave them with a positive impression, affirming that you're a well-rounded candidate. So, how do you approach this? Here are some guidelines.

Firstly, understand that there's no singular right response. Feel free to talk about your passions, whether that's engaging in community service, exploring new destinations, enhancing your skills through evening courses, or any hobby that speaks to your character. The key is to convey aspects of your life that illustrate you're engaging, well-balanced, and a positive addition to their team.

Keep your explanation brief. If birdwatching is your hobby, for instance, a concise, enthusiastic overview is more effective than an exhaustive list of every bird you've spotted. This shows your enthusiasm without risking the impression that you lack conciseness or are overly anxious.

Lastly, tread carefully around sensitive topics. It might seem straightforward, but "inappropriate" can extend to anything excessively divisive, such as political affiliations or religious beliefs, beyond the obvious like risky or legally dubious activities. It's about being mindful not to alienate any member of your audience.

This question is a chance to highlight your multifaceted personality. Embrace it, showcasing how your personal interests complement your professional qualifications.

### Where do you see yourself in five years?

Addressing the question of where you envision yourself in five years during an interview can be daunting for many, a perfectly understandable sentiment given the unpredictability of life and career paths. However, the secret to effectively responding lies in shifting the focus towards what you can contribute to the company and the specific position. Let's explore this through three actionable suggestions.

Firstly, segment your response into intervals of two to three years. This structuring allows the interviewer to clearly grasp your plans and ambitions. Outline what you aim to achieve in the initial two to three years, followed by your aspirations for the subsequent period.

Secondly, emphasize the overarching goals you have for your tenure in the role and the impact you aim to make during these phases. It's about conveying the value you intend to bring to the company, rather than just personal milestones.

Thirdly, it's wise to avoid fixating on specific job titles you aspire to attain within that timeframe, as this might appear presumptuous or overly ambitious.

In summary, by dividing your response into manageable phases, concentrating on the contributions you plan to make, and steering clear of title-focused aspirations, you'll navigate this common interview question with confidence and clarity.

### "Do you have any questions?"

This inquiry came up after a standout applicant of mine had completed their interview, and the feedback I received was unexpectedly disheartening. They were deemed disengaged for not having questions at the interview's conclusion. That candidate's response of "no" to the pivotal query of whether they had any questions signaled a lack of interest, costing them the opportunity.

Answering affirmatively to this question is non-negotiable. It's a litmus test for your enthusiasm, intellect, and engagement, presenting a chance to leave a memorable impression. So, what should you inquire about? Consider these categories:

- Demonstrate active listening by revisiting topics discussed during the interview. This could involve asking for more details on specific job duties, the team, or upcoming challenges.

- Express genuine enthusiasm by asking about the company's products, branding, or industry trends, illustrating your passion and potential fit within their culture.

- Engage them on their professional journey. People enjoy discussing their accomplishments and career paths. Inquire about how their experiences have shaped their current roles, but maintain professionalism and avoid overly personal questions.

Asking thoughtful questions not only showcases your interest but also builds rapport, enhancing your likability and fittingness for the position.

### Can you describe a moment when you exceeded expectations?

Answering questions about previous experiences or those that prompt you to recall specific instances in interviews hinges on your ability to craft and narrate a compelling story. We, as people, are inherently captivated by stories, making this approach a powerful tool to pique an employer's interest in you.

Begin your narrative by setting the scene, akin to the opening of a gripping film. Outline the circumstances and challenges you faced in four sentences or so, laying a solid foundation for your story. This part is crucial as it sets the stage for your actions.

Next, detail the actions you took, focusing on the pivotal steps. Keep this segment concise, around two to three sentences, utilizing dynamic verbs to convey your initiative—words like "executed" or "negotiated" add life to your actions.

Conclude with the outcome of your efforts, aiming to leave a lasting impression with a memorable ending that underscores your achievement.

To succinctly frame your response to such inquiries about past experiences, remember the SAR technique: Situation, Action, Results. This structure will guide you in articulating responses to various types of experience-based interview questions effectively.

### How to handle past experience questions

Navigating questions about previous experiences during interviews is pivotal, and engaging storytelling is your best ally. Our affinity for absorbing captivating narratives means that a well-told tale about your professional journey can significantly boost your appeal to potential employers.

Begin with a clear depiction of the context, similar to setting the scene in a compelling narrative. Elaborate on the initial situation, highlighting the challenges faced. This foundational aspect of your story is critical and should extend over three to four sentences.

Next, delve into the actions you undertook, focusing on significant phases without overloading on details. Aim for brevity, around two to three sentences, and employ dynamic action words such as "executed" or "influenced" to bring energy to your recount.

Conclude with the impact of your actions, ideally anchoring your narrative with a strong ending that showcases tangible achievements, like cost reductions or enhancements in efficiency.

To effectively structure responses to inquiries about your past experiences, employ the SAR (Situation, Action, Results) method. This framework ensures a coherent and impactful delivery, enabling you to tackle any experiential question with confidence.

# MAP OF THE CYBERSECURITY INTERVIEWS

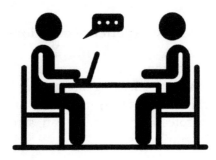

Discussing the overarching structure of the interview process, we begin with the initial phase, which is centered on conducting thorough research and compiling information that sets you apart from other candidates. As you move into the intermediate stage, the focus shifts towards logistical arrangements, addressing queries, and honing your communication skills. The concluding phase is about patience and learning—though it may appear as a period of inactivity, your engagement and follow-up strategies can significantly influence an employer's decision in your favor, assuming all other qualifications are on par.

Exploring three distinct stages of the interview process reveals the importance of preparation in ensuring a successful outcome. A critical aspect of this preparation is gaining insight into your audience's interests and the factors they deem important. Identifying the key players—HR, management, and peers—helps tailor your approach to meet their specific expectations, as each group evaluates candidates based on different criteria, though some may intersect.

HR's role is to assess your compatibility with the company's ethos, focusing on behavioral tendencies and potential to contribute positively to the company's goals. While HR may inquire about role-specific knowledge, their primary concern is not technical expertise, so responses should be concise, emphasizing your alignment with the company's values.

Conversely, supervisors and managers delve into the technical aspects of the position, evaluating your practical skills and how you articulate your experiences. They also consider personality fit with the team, making it crucial to listen actively for team challenges and highlight relevant achievements.

Peer interviews, while potentially technical, aim to evaluate your team dynamics and problem-solving approach with colleagues. Although your technical skills have been vetted by management, peers focus on your interpersonal skills and teamwork, inviting stories that showcase your collaborative spirit and conflict resolution abilities.

In summary, navigating the interview process successfully involves understanding the distinct perspectives of HR, management, and peers, and strategically addressing each group's unique criteria.

Cybersecurity roles are undeniably technical in nature, demanding a firm grasp on network security and firewall implementation among other foundational skills. In interviews for such positions, while initial questions might explore your aspirations and unique aspects not listed on your resume, the focus inevitably shifts towards assessing your technical proficiency.

Equally, while soft and interpersonal skills hold their value, the essence of cybersecurity roles lies in the depth of your technical understanding.

This emphasis on technical expertise should be a guiding principle as you prepare for a cybersecurity interview. Possessing relevant experience in cybersecurity or network engineering becomes particularly pivotal for those eyeing entry and mid-level positions.

Demonstrating a comprehensive understanding of the industry and its various segments can significantly bolster your candidacy, showcasing your commitment to professional growth and your capability to align with the company's strategic goals.

### Emphasizing Passion and Professional Growth

True passion for cybersecurity, beyond merely stating it, can be discerned by hiring managers. Demonstrating this through mentions of relevant courses, internships, or certifications on your resume and discussing these experiences during the interview can set you apart.

### Understanding the Cybersecurity Job Hierarchy

The cybersecurity field features a diverse range of titles, some synonymous and others distinct yet similar in function. Here's a snapshot of the typical career ladder within the sector, though variations exist globally.

At the entry-level, positions might include titles like Cyber Security intern (Entry-Level), Cybersecurity Apprentice, and Junior Cybersecurity Associate.

For those contributing individually, titles could be IT Analyst, Cybersecurity Analyst, SOC Analyst, Penetration Tester, Security Engineer, Cryptographer, Cloud Architect, Data Security Analyst, or Cybersecurity Technician.

Advancing to a managerial role, you might find yourself as an IT Manager, with titles under this category including Distribution

Manager, Production Manager, and Quality Assurance Manager (QA).

The next tier up is the IT Director, encompassing roles such as Cybersecurity Leader or Team Leader, Cybersecurity Director, or Director of Information Security.

Ascending further, the Vice President of Cybersecurity position encompasses roles like Cybersecurity Executive or Security Executive.

At the pinnacle is the Chief Information Security Officer (CISO), also known as Chief Security Officer, Head of Cybersecurity, or President of Cybersecurity, representing the zenith of the cybersecurity career path.

## GENERAL GUIDELINES AND PREPARATION FOR THE INTERVIEW

Approaching a cybersecurity job interview requires a nuanced strategy that balances demonstrating technical expertise, understanding of the cybersecurity landscape, and soft skills like communication and problem-solving. Given the critical importance of cybersecurity in protecting organizations' digital assets, candidates must showcase not only their technical acumen but also their adaptability, continuous learning attitude, and ability to think like an attacker. Here's a comprehensive guide on how to approach a cybersecurity job interview:

### 1. Technical Preparation

Understand the Basics and Beyond: Ensure you have a strong grasp of cybersecurity fundamentals such as encryption, network security, firewall configuration, intrusion detection systems, and the latest security threats and vulnerabilities. Advanced understanding in areas specific to the job you're applying for, such as cloud security, penetration testing, or incident response, can set you apart.

**Stay Updated**: Cybersecurity is a rapidly evolving field. Familiarize yourself with the latest trends, threats, technologies, and best practices. Being able to discuss recent high-profile cyber attacks or emerging technologies like AI in cybersecurity demonstrates your engagement with the industry.

**Practical Experience**: Hands-on experience is invaluable. Whether through previous jobs, internships, personal projects, or labs, be prepared to discuss real-world applications of your skills. Highlight specific tools and technologies you're proficient with, and be ready to discuss how you've used them in practical scenarios.

### 2. Soft Skills and Problem-Solving

**Communication**: Cybersecurity professionals often need to explain complex concepts to non-technical stakeholders. Practice explaining technical details in a clear, concise manner. You may be asked to describe how you would communicate a security breach to senior management or train staff on security awareness.

**Critical Thinking**: Be prepared to tackle hypothetical scenarios or problem-solving exercises that assess your analytical skills and approach to tackling security challenges. Demonstrating a methodical approach to identifying, analyzing, and addressing security issues is crucial.

**Teamwork and Leadership**: Cybersecurity is rarely a solo effort. Highlight experiences where you've collaborated with others, led a team, or contributed to a group project. Discuss how you handle conflicts, share knowledge, and motivate team members.

### CYBERSECURITY CERTIFICATIONS IN INTERVIEWS

When navigating the journey of a cybersecurity interview, certifications play a crucial role in showcasing your expertise, dedication, and commitment to the field. The relevance of certifications in cybersecurity cannot be overstated; they serve as a benchmark of your skills and knowledge, providing a tangible testament to your ability to meet industry standards. Understanding how to effectively present and leverage your certifications during an interview can significantly impact your candidacy. Here's an extensive guide on the relevance of certifications and how to present them when facing a cybersecurity interview.

## The Relevance of Certifications in Cybersecurity

Validation of Skills: Certifications are a third-party endorsement of your cybersecurity skills and knowledge. They validate that you have met specific criteria and mastered certain competencies as defined by industry standards.

Keeping Pace with the Industry: Cybersecurity is a rapidly evolving field. Certifications demonstrate your commitment to staying updated with the latest technologies, threats, and best practices.

Meeting Employer Expectations: Many organizations view certifications as essential requirements for cybersecurity roles. They can be seen as a prerequisite for more advanced positions or certain specializations within cybersecurity.

Competitive Advantage: Holding relevant certifications can distinguish you from other candidates who may have similar experience levels but lack formal recognition of their skills.

## How to Present Certifications in an Interview

Tailor to the Job Description: Highlight certifications that are most relevant to the job you're applying for. If the job listing specifically mentions certifications like CISSP, CEH, or CompTIA Security+, make sure to discuss them prominently.

Explain the Value: Don't just list your certifications; explain what they mean in terms of your capabilities. Discuss the skills and knowledge you gained through the certification process and how they apply to the position you're interviewing for.

Share Your Learning Journey: Employers are interested in how you approach challenges and your commitment to continuous learning. Share stories about why you pursued certain certifications, the challenges you overcame to achieve them, and how they have contributed to your professional growth.

Connect to Real-World Applications: Provide examples of how the expertise validated by your certifications has been applied in real-world scenarios. Discuss specific projects or challenges where your certified skills made a difference.

Future Plans: Cybersecurity requires lifelong learning. Discuss any certifications you are currently pursuing or plan to obtain in the future. This demonstrates your initiative to expand your skills proactively.

## ONLINE PRACTICE PLATFORMS AND HOW TO USE THEM IN YOUR FAVOR

When preparing for a cybersecurity interview, showcasing your practical experience, including participation in online labs like Hack The Box or TryHackMe, is highly relevant and can significantly enhance your candidacy. These platforms offer hands-on experience with real-world scenarios, allowing you to apply theoretical knowledge in practical settings. This section delves into the importance of such experiences and how to effectively present them during a cybersecurity interview.

### Importance of Practical Experience in Cybersecurity

Bridging Theory and Practice: Cybersecurity is a field where theoretical knowledge needs to be complemented with practical skills. Online labs provide a controlled environment to experiment with different tools, techniques, and strategies, bridging the gap between theory and real-world application.

Demonstrating Problem-Solving Skills: Success in cybersecurity requires an aptitude for problem-solving. Completing challenges on platforms like Hack The Box or TryHackMe showcases your ability to think critically and persistently address complex security issues.

Staying Updated with Latest Threats: These platforms often update their scenarios to reflect current cybersecurity threats, ensuring that your skills remain relevant to the ever-evolving threat landscape.

Showing Initiative and Self-Directed Learning: Engaging with these platforms demonstrates a proactive approach to your professional development, highlighting your dedication to staying ahead in the field.

### Presenting Online Lab Experiences in Interviews

Highlight Specific Achievements: Mention any particularly challenging boxes or labs you've completed and what you learned from them. Discuss any rankings or achievements that underscore your proficiency and dedication.

Relate Experiences to Job Requirements: Draw direct connections between the skills and knowledge you've gained through online labs and the job description. This can involve discussing specific security tools you've mastered, attack methodologies you're familiar with, or particular vulnerabilities you've learned to exploit and defend against.

Discuss Learning Outcomes: Focus on what these experiences have taught you beyond just technical skills. This can include lessons in time management, research methods, or collaboration with others in the cybersecurity community.

### Tips for Effectively Integrating Online Lab Experiences into Your Interview

Prepare a Portfolio: Consider creating a digital portfolio that showcases your achievements on these platforms. This can include certificates, badges, or a summary of your rankings and completed challenges.

Stay Concise and Relevant: While it's important to highlight your practical experience, ensure your explanations are concise and directly relevant to the interviewer's questions.

Update Your Resume: Include a section on your resume dedicated to practical experiences, highlighting your participation in platforms like Hack The Box or TryHackMe, especially if you've achieved notable rankings or completed significant challenges.

Practice Explaining Technical Concepts: Be prepared to explain complex technical concepts in simple terms. This not only demonstrates your technical knowledge but also your ability to communicate effectively, a key skill in cybersecurity roles.

# HOW TO TACKLE THE INTERVIEW IF YOU HAVE NOT PREVIOUS WORK EXPERIENCE IN CYBERSECURITY

Facing a cybersecurity interview without direct work experience can be daunting, yet it's entirely possible to turn this situation into an opportunity to showcase your potential. The cybersecurity field values practical skills, theoretical knowledge, and a demonstrable passion for the subject. Here's an extensive guide on how to approach a cybersecurity interview when you lack formal work experience.

### Emphasize Education and Certifications

Highlight Relevant Education: If you've completed any formal education related to cybersecurity, computer science, or information technology, make sure to highlight this. Discuss specific courses that are relevant to the job you're applying for and how they have prepared you for a career in cybersecurity.

Certifications Can Be Key: Certifications such as CompTIA Security+, CEH (Certified Ethical Hacker), or (ISC)² SSCP (Systems Security Certified Practitioner) demonstrate your commitment and knowledge. Even if you're in the process of obtaining a certification, mention it to show your initiative in professional development.

### Showcase Practical Experience

Leverage Labs and Simulations: Hands-on experience gained through platforms like Hack The Box, TryHackMe, or through personal projects can be incredibly valuable. Discuss the challenges you've completed, what you've learned, and how these experiences have equipped you with practical cybersecurity skills.

**Participation in CTFs** (Capture The Flag) Competitions: If you've participated in any cybersecurity competitions, share your experiences. These competitions are excellent for demonstrating your problem-solving skills, technical abilities, and how you perform under pressure.

### Demonstrate Soft Skills and Potential

Problem-Solving Skills: Cybersecurity is all about solving complex problems. Share examples from your personal or academic life where you've successfully tackled difficult challenges.

Continuous Learning: Express your dedication to staying updated with the latest in cybersecurity. Mention blogs, podcasts, webinars, and conferences you follow or attend to keep abreast of new threats and technologies.

Adaptability: The ability to adapt to new situations and learn quickly is crucial in cybersecurity. Provide examples of how you've had to learn new technologies or concepts swiftly and apply them effectively.

### Highlight Transferable Skills

From Unrelated Work Experience: Even if your previous jobs weren't in cybersecurity, they might have taught you valuable skills. Customer service roles, for example, develop your communication skills, while working in teams can highlight your ability to collaborate.

Volunteer Work and Internships: Any volunteer work or internships, especially those related to IT or cybersecurity, should be mentioned. These experiences can provide a foundation of practical skills and demonstrate your work ethic and commitment.

Lack of work experience doesn't have to be a barrier to entering the cybersecurity field. By effectively showcasing your education, certifications, practical skills, and soft skills, you can demonstrate your potential to be a valuable asset to any cybersecurity team. The key is to frame your existing experiences, no matter how unrelated they may seem, in a way that highlights your readiness and eagerness to embark on a cybersecurity career. Remember, your passion for the field, combined with a proactive approach to learning and skill development, can make a strong impression on potential employers.

## CYBERSECURITY INTERVIEW WITH PREVIOUS WORK EXPERIENCE IN SERVICE DESK OR SIMILAR ENTRY-LEVEL JOBS

Transitioning from a service desk or IT technician role to a cybersecurity position is a path many professionals take. Your experience in these roles can provide a solid foundation for a career in cybersecurity, given the overlap in technical skills, problem-solving abilities, and understanding of IT infrastructure. Here's how to tackle a cybersecurity interview with your background:

### Leverage Your Technical Foundation

Highlight Relevant Skills: Service desk and IT technician roles develop a deep understanding of hardware, software, and network troubleshooting. Emphasize how this knowledge equips you to understand the technical underpinnings of cybersecurity threats and defenses.

Discuss Experience with Security Issues: If you've dealt with security-related incidents, such as malware infections, phishing attempts, or unauthorized access, describe your role in identifying, mitigating, and resolving these issues. This demonstrates your practical experience in handling security incidents.

### Showcase Your Problem-Solving Skills

Real-world Problem Solving: Use specific examples from your work history to illustrate your problem-solving skills. Explain the steps you took to diagnose and resolve complex technical issues, highlighting any instances where you improved processes or implemented preventive measures to enhance security.

Analytical Thinking: Cybersecurity requires the ability to analyze data and recognize patterns that could indicate security breaches. Discuss how your role required analytical skills, such as parsing logs, monitoring system performance, or assessing network traffic, and how these skills are transferable to cybersecurity.

### Demonstrate Your Ability to Learn and Adapt

Continuous Learning: Cybersecurity is a rapidly evolving field. Discuss how you've kept your skills up-to-date or expanded your knowledge base. This could include formal training, certifications (CompTIA Network+, CompTIA Security+, etc.), self-study, or participation in relevant projects.

Adaptability: IT roles demand adaptability to changing technologies and situations. Share examples of how you've adapted to new systems, software, or protocols, underscoring your capacity to grow within the cybersecurity domain.

## CYBERSECURITY INTERVIEW: FROM SECURITY ANALYST TO SECURITY ENGINEER

Transitioning from a security analyst to a cybersecurity engineer role represents a significant step forward in one's career. This move often entails a deeper dive into the technical aspects of cybersecurity, including the design, implementation, and management of security solutions to protect against threats. With previous experience as a security analyst, you're already familiar with assessing and mitigating vulnerabilities, which serves as a solid foundation for moving into an engineering role. Here's how to approach a cybersecurity interview when you're aiming to make this transition:

### Leverage Your Analytical Experience

Showcase Your Analytical Skills: Begin by highlighting your experience as a security analyst, emphasizing your ability to identify, evaluate, and mitigate risks. Explain how this has provided you with a keen understanding of the threat landscape and the technical prowess to think like an attacker, which is crucial for an engineering role.

**Detail Your Technical Experience**: Discuss the tools, technologies, and methodologies you've used in your role as a security analyst. Be specific about any security software you're proficient in, types of malware you've analyzed, or incidents you've responded to. This will demonstrate your hands-on experience and familiarity with the technical side of cybersecurity.

### Emphasize Project and Implementation Experience

Discuss Security Solutions: Talk about any involvement you've had in selecting, configuring, or implementing security solutions. Highlight your understanding of different security architectures and controls, and your ability to integrate them into an existing IT infrastructure.

Highlight Project Management Skills: If you've led or played a key role in security-related projects, detail your responsibilities and the outcomes. Discuss how you managed timelines, coordinated with stakeholders, and achieved project goals. This experience is valuable for a cybersecurity engineer who will often lead projects to enhance an organization's security posture.

### Upgrade Your Technical Knowledge

Pursue Advanced Certifications: While you may already hold certifications relevant to a security analyst role (such as CompTIA Security+, CEH, or GSEC), consider pursuing more advanced certifications that align with cybersecurity engineering (like CISSP, OSCP, or specialized certifications in cloud security, for example). Mention any certifications you're working towards or planning to pursue.

Stay Current with Technology Trends: Cybersecurity engineering roles often require a deeper understanding of emerging technologies and their security implications. Demonstrate your knowledge of recent developments in cybersecurity, such as cloud security, zero trust architectures, or AI and machine learning in threat detection.

Moving from a security analyst to a cybersecurity engineer role is a natural progression for many cybersecurity professionals. By effectively leveraging your analytical experience, highlighting your involvement in security projects, upgrading your technical knowledge, and demonstrating your soft skills and leadership abilities, you can make a compelling case for your transition during the interview. Remember, the goal is to show not only that you have the necessary background and skills but also that you're proactive about growing and taking on more complex and technical responsibilities in the field of cybersecurity.

## CYBERSECURITY INTERVIEW: FROM SECURITY ENGINEER TO SECURITY ARCHITECT

Transitioning from a cybersecurity engineer to an architect role is a significant career step, involving a shift from hands-on technical work to designing and overseeing the implementation of comprehensive security strategies and architectures. This move requires not only a deep technical foundation but also strategic thinking, leadership skills, and a broad understanding of business processes and IT infrastructure. Here's how to approach a cybersecurity interview when aiming for an architect role:

### Demonstrate Strategic Vision and Understanding

Broad Technical Knowledge: Highlight your comprehensive technical knowledge gained as a security engineer. Emphasize your understanding of various cybersecurity technologies, frameworks, and standards, as well as how they integrate into an overall security architecture.

Strategic Thinking: Showcase your ability to think strategically about cybersecurity. Discuss how you have identified long-term security threats and developed strategies to mitigate them. Architects need to see the big picture and plan accordingly, so highlight any experience you have in developing or contributing to cybersecurity strategy.

### Highlight Leadership and Communication Skills

Leadership Experience: Even if you haven't held a formal leadership position, discuss any instances where you led a project, mentored junior engineers, or influenced decision-making processes. Cybersecurity architects often lead teams and need to inspire confidence in their vision and strategy.

Effective Communication: Cybersecurity architects must communicate complex security concepts to stakeholders across the organization. Share examples of how you've effectively communicated security risks and solutions to non-technical audiences, including senior management.

Transitioning from a cybersecurity engineer to an architect role is a significant career step, involving a shift from hands-on technical work to designing and overseeing the implementation of comprehensive security strategies and architectures. This move requires not only a deep technical foundation but also strategic thinking, leadership skills, and a broad understanding of business processes and IT infrastructure. Here's how to approach a cybersecurity interview when aiming for an architect role:

### Demonstrate Strategic Vision and Understanding

Broad Technical Knowledge: Highlight your comprehensive technical knowledge gained as a security engineer. Emphasize your understanding of various cybersecurity technologies, frameworks, and standards, as well as how they integrate into an overall security architecture.

Strategic Thinking: Showcase your ability to think strategically about cybersecurity. Discuss how you have identified long-term security threats and developed strategies to mitigate them. Architects need to see the big picture and plan accordingly, so highlight any experience you have in developing or contributing to cybersecurity strategy.

### Highlight Leadership and Communication Skills

Leadership Experience: Even if you haven't held a formal leadership position, discuss any instances where you led a project, mentored junior engineers, or influenced decision-making processes. Cybersecurity architects often lead teams and need to inspire confidence in their vision and strategy.

Effective Communication: Cybersecurity architects must communicate complex security concepts to stakeholders across the organization. Share examples of how you've effectively communicated security risks and solutions to non-technical audiences, including senior management.

## Showcase Project and Risk Management Skills

Project Management: Describe your involvement in managing security projects, including planning, execution, and monitoring. Highlight your ability to deliver projects on time and within budget while achieving security objectives.

Risk Management: Discuss your experience with risk assessment methodologies and your approach to balancing security needs with business objectives. Architects need to prioritize risks and allocate resources efficiently, so provide examples of how you've achieved this.

## Emphasize Architectural Design Experience

Security Solutions Design: If you have experience designing security solutions or contributing to the security architecture, detail these projects. Discuss how you ensured the solutions were scalable, cost-effective, and aligned with business goals.

Understanding of Enterprise Architecture: Demonstrate your understanding of how cybersecurity integrates with the broader IT and enterprise architecture. If you have experience with enterprise architecture frameworks (e.g., TOGAF, Zachman), mention this.

## Continuous Learning and Professional Development

Stay Updated: Cybersecurity is a rapidly evolving field. Discuss how you stay informed about the latest security trends, threats, and technologies. This could include attending conferences, obtaining certifications, or participating in professional groups.

Advanced Certifications: Holding advanced certifications (e.g.,

CISSP, CISM, SABSA) can be particularly beneficial for architect roles. If you have these certifications, discuss what you learned and how they're relevant to your career aspirations. If you're working towards any, mention your plans.

## CYBERSECURITY INTERVIEW: FROM SECURITY ARCHITECT TO SECURITY MANAGER

Transitioning from a cybersecurity architect to a security manager role involves a strategic shift from focusing primarily on designing and implementing security architectures to overseeing a security program, managing a team, and aligning security initiatives with business objectives. This step up the career ladder requires not only a solid foundation in cybersecurity principles but also strong leadership, communication, and strategic planning skills. Here's how to tackle a cybersecurity interview when aiming for a security manager position:

### Emphasize Leadership and Management Skills

Leadership Experience: Highlight any experience you have leading teams, managing projects, or influencing security policy. Discuss how you have motivated and guided teams towards achieving security and business goals.

Management Capabilities: Detail your experience with budgeting, resource allocation, and program management. Security managers are often responsible for managing the security budget and resources, so demonstrate your ability to efficiently utilize resources to maximize security posture.

Conflict Resolution: Share examples of how you've successfully navigated disagreements or conflicts, either within your team or with other stakeholders. Being able to balance different interests and find common ground is crucial for a security manager.

### Demonstrate Strategic Planning and Execution

Strategic Vision: Discuss how you've contributed to the development and implementation of security strategies in your role as an architect. Highlight your ability to align security strategies with broader business objectives, a key responsibility for security managers.

Risk Management: Explain your approach to identifying, assessing, and mitigating risks. Provide examples of how you've balanced risk against business needs, prioritizing resources and initiatives to protect critical assets.

Compliance and Standards: Detail your experience ensuring compliance with industry standards and regulatory requirements. Security managers need to navigate the complex landscape of compliance while maintaining an effective security posture.

### Showcase Communication and Interpersonal Skills

Stakeholder Engagement: Share examples of how you've worked with stakeholders across the organization to promote security awareness and foster a culture of security. Security managers need to communicate effectively with stakeholders at all levels, from technical teams to executive leadership.

Training and Development: Discuss your experience developing and delivering security training programs. As a security manager, you'll be responsible for ensuring your team and the wider organization are equipped with the knowledge and skills to maintain security.

Crisis Management: Provide examples of how you've handled security incidents or crises. Being able to lead calmly and effectively during a crisis is a critical skill for security managers.

### Highlight Your Technical Foundation

Technical Expertise: While the role of a security manager is more strategic and less hands-on, a deep understanding of cybersecurity technologies and principles is still essential. Highlight your technical background and how it informs your strategic decisions.

Up-to-Date Knowledge: Cybersecurity is a rapidly evolving field. Discuss how you stay current with the latest security threats, trends, and technologies, demonstrating your commitment to continuous learning.

## ESSENTIAL BASIS YOU SHOULD BE FAMILIAR WITH

Facing a job interview in cybersecurity demands a broad understanding of various areas within the field, given its complexity and the diverse range of threats that organizations encounter. Cybersecurity encompasses multiple domains, each crucial for protecting information assets against increasingly sophisticated cyber threats. Here's an extensive overview of key areas you should be familiar with to effectively prepare for a cybersecurity job interview:

### 1. Cybersecurity Fundamentals

Understanding of Basic Concepts: Know the core principles of confidentiality, integrity, and availability (CIA triad), as well as the basics of encryption, authentication, and authorization. Understanding these foundational concepts is critical for any role within cybersecurity.

### 2. Network Security

Network Architectures and Protocols: A solid grasp of how networks are structured (LAN, WAN, VPN, etc.) and an understanding of key protocols (TCP/IP, HTTP, HTTPS, SMTP, etc.) are essential. This includes knowledge of how data moves across the network and the potential vulnerabilities at each step.

Firewalls and Intrusion Detection Systems (IDS): Know how

firewalls and IDS/IPS (Intrusion Prevention Systems) function to protect networks from unauthorized access and monitoring for malicious activity.

### 3. Application Security

Secure Coding Practices: Understanding common vulnerabilities in web applications (such as SQL injection, cross-site scripting, etc.) and best practices for secure coding is crucial, especially for roles focused on application security.

Web Application Firewalls (WAFs): Knowledge of how WAFs protect web applications by filtering and monitoring HTTP traffic between a web application and the Internet.

### 4. Endpoint Security

Malware and Antivirus Solutions: Be familiar with different types of malware (viruses, worms, trojans, ransomware, etc.) and how antivirus solutions and endpoint protection platforms work to detect and neutralize threats.

Patch Management: Understanding the importance of regular software updates and patch management as a defense against exploits targeting software vulnerabilities.

### 5. Identity and Access Management (IAM)

Authentication Mechanisms: Knowledge of various authentication methods (passwords, multi-factor authentication, biometrics, etc.) and their application in securing access to systems and data.

Privileged Access Management: The principles of least privilege and the management of privileged accounts to reduce the risk of unauthorized access to critical systems.

### 6. Cloud Security

Cloud Service Models: Understand the security implications of different cloud service models (IaaS, PaaS, SaaS) and how responsibility for security is shared between the cloud provider and the customer.

Cloud Security Best Practices: Familiarity with cloud security frameworks and best practices, including data encryption, identity management, and secure API integration.

### 7. Incident Response and Recovery

Incident Response Plans: Knowledge of how to prepare for, detect, respond to, and recover from security incidents. Understanding the roles and responsibilities in an incident response team.

Disaster Recovery and Business Continuity: The principles of disaster recovery planning and business continuity management to ensure that operations can continue in the event of a significant incident.

### 8. Legal and Regulatory Compliance

Understanding Compliance Requirements: Awareness of key cybersecurity regulations (GDPR, HIPAA, CCPA, etc.) and standards (ISO 27001, NIST frameworks, etc.) that organizations must comply with.

Ethical and Legal Considerations: The ethical implications of cybersecurity practices, including privacy concerns and the legal consequences of security breaches.

**Research the Specific Role**: Cybersecurity roles can vary widely, so tailor your preparation to the specific position you're interviewing for. Review the job description to identify the key areas of focus.

**Stay Updated:** Cybersecurity is a rapidly evolving field. Stay informed about the latest threats, technologies, and best practices by following industry news, attending webinars, and participating in relevant forums and conferences.

**Prepare Examples**: Be ready to discuss specific examples from your experience or studies that demonstrate your knowledge and skills in these areas. Real-world applications of your knowledge will be particularly compelling to interviewers.

## SOFT SKILLS AND COMPETENCIES

### Effective Communication in Cybersecurity

In the realm of cybersecurity, where the complexity of technical challenges meets the necessity for clear, concise, and effective communication, the ability to articulate thoughts and findings becomes invaluable. This section delves into why effective communication is paramount in cybersecurity roles and how you can showcase this critical skill during your job interview.

### The Importance of Communication in Cybersecurity

Cybersecurity professionals operate at the intersection of technology, business, and user interaction. Their role often involves explaining intricate security concepts to non-technical stakeholders, writing reports that clearly outline risks and recommendations, and collaborating with team members to resolve security incidents. Thus, effective communication is not just a supplementary skill but a cornerstone of successful cybersecurity practice.

### 1. Bridging the Gap Between Technical and Non-Technical Audiences

Understanding Your Audience: Tailor your language and examples based on the audience's technical understanding. For stakeholders, focus on the implications of security issues on business objectives rather than the technical details.

Simplifying Complex Concepts: Use analogies and simple language to explain technical security threats or measures. Avoid jargon and acronyms that might alienate or confuse the listener.

## 2. Reporting and Documentation

Clarity and Precision: Whether drafting a security policy or documenting an incident report, the clarity of your writing directly impacts its effectiveness. Practice writing concise, action-oriented sentences that convey essential information without ambiguity.

Structured Reporting: Learn to structure your documents logically, with clear headings, bullet points, and summaries. This organization helps readers quickly find the information they need.

## 3. Verbal Communication in Team Settings

Active Listening: Effective communication is as much about listening as it is about speaking. Show your ability to listen actively by summarizing points made by others and asking clarifying questions.

Articulating Ideas: Practice articulating your thoughts and ideas clearly and confidently in team meetings or discussions. Being able to voice your opinions and contributions is crucial for collaborative problem-solving.

## 4. Presentation Skills

Conveying Confidence: When presenting, your posture, eye contact, and voice modulation can significantly impact how your message is received. Practice speaking in front of a mirror or record yourself to improve your delivery.

Engaging Your Audience: Learn to engage your audience with questions, interactive elements, or relatable examples, especially when explaining cybersecurity risks or training staff on security awareness.

## Demonstrating Effective Communication During Your Interview

Prepare Concise Answers: When responding to interview questions, structure your answers clearly. Start with a brief overview, provide necessary details, and conclude with a summary or key takeaway.

Share Real-Life Examples: Illustrate your communication skills by sharing real-life scenarios where you effectively communicated complex information to non-technical staff or led a team through a security challenge.

Ask Thoughtful Questions: The questions you ask during the interview can also demonstrate your communication skills. Prepare insightful questions that show you've researched the company and thought deeply about the role you're applying for.

# THE CYBERSECURITY INTERVIEW PROCESS

Understanding the Typical Structure of Cybersecurity Interviews

The interview process for a cybersecurity position can be both exciting and daunting. Given the critical importance of cybersecurity roles in protecting an organization's data and systems, the interview process is designed to rigorously assess a candidate's technical abilities, problem-solving skills, and cultural fit. Understanding the typical structure of these interviews can significantly help candidates prepare and perform effectively. This section explores the common stages and components of the cybersecurity interview process.

## 1. Initial Screening

Purpose: The initial screening, often conducted via phone or video call, aims to verify the candidate's basic qualifications, career objectives, and interest in the role. It's typically handled by HR or a recruiter.

Preparation Tips: Be ready to discuss your resume, explain why you're interested in the role, and briefly touch on your relevant experience and certifications. It's also a good opportunity to demonstrate your communication skills.

### 2. Technical Interview

Purpose: This stage dives deeper into the candidate's technical expertise and problem-solving capabilities. It may be conducted by a senior cybersecurity team member or a technical panel and can include practical assessments, technical questions, or case studies.

Preparation Tips: Brush up on fundamental cybersecurity concepts, tools, and best practices. Be prepared to discuss past projects or experiences in detail, and possibly participate in live problem-solving scenarios or technical demonstrations.

### 3. Behavioral Interview

Purpose: The focus here is on the candidate's soft skills, cultural fit, and how they handle specific situations. Questions are often framed as "Tell me about a time when..." to elicit examples of past behavior.

Preparation Tips: Reflect on various challenges and accomplishments in your career, especially those that showcase leadership, teamwork, adaptability, and communication. Use the STAR method (Situation, Task, Action, Result) to structure your responses.

### 4. Managerial or Team Fit Interview

Purpose: Candidates may meet with potential direct managers or team members to assess how well they would integrate with the team and contribute to its dynamics. This stage evaluates the candidate's alignment with the team's working style, values, and goals.

Preparation Tips: Show genuine interest in the team's work and ask insightful questions about their projects, challenges, and team culture. Be yourself, and share examples that illustrate your ability to collaborate and contribute to a positive work environment.

### 5. Presentation or Case Study

Purpose: For some roles, candidates may be asked to prepare a presentation or complete a case study relevant to the position. This assesses the candidate's ability to analyze information, devise strategies, and communicate complex ideas effectively.

Preparation Tips: Ensure your presentation or case study solution is well-structured, clearly articulated, and demonstrates your analytical skills. Practice presenting to friends or colleagues to refine **your delivery and receive feedback.**

6. Final Interview with Leadership

Purpose: This last step often involves an interview with higher management or cybersecurity leadership. The focus is on gauging the candidate's potential for growth, leadership abilities, and strategic thinking.

Preparation Tips: Be prepared to discuss your long-term career aspirations, how you see yourself contributing to the organization's security posture, and your thoughts on the future of cybersecurity.

## TECHNICAL INTERVIEWS: WHAT TO EXPECT AND HOW TO PREPARE

Technical interviews are a crucial component of the hiring

process for cybersecurity roles. They provide employers with a direct insight into your technical skills, problem-solving abilities, and suitability for the specific demands of the role. Understanding what to expect and how to prepare can significantly enhance your performance in these interviews.

**What to Expect**

1. In-Depth Technical Questions: Expect questions that probe your understanding of cybersecurity principles, technologies, and practices. These can range from theoretical questions about security models and encryption algorithms to practical inquiries regarding firewall configurations, incident response procedures, and vulnerability assessment tools.

2. Practical Assessments and Simulations: Many employers incorporate practical exercises to evaluate your hands-on skills. This may involve analyzing logs to identify suspicious activities, performing live penetration testing on a controlled environment, or identifying vulnerabilities in a piece of code.

3. Scenario-Based Questions: Employers often use hypothetical scenarios to understand how you would react in real-world situations. You might be asked to describe how you would handle a specific security breach, mitigate a DDoS attack, or implement a security policy across an organization.

4. Discussion of Past Projects: Be prepared to discuss previous projects or roles in detail, focusing on your contributions, the technologies you used, the challenges you faced, and the outcomes. This helps interviewers gauge your experience level and how you approach and resolve complex issues.

**How to Prepare**

1. Review Core Cybersecurity Concepts: Ensure you have a strong grasp of fundamental cybersecurity concepts, such as encryption, network security, application security, and threat intelligence.

Understanding current trends and emerging threats is also crucial.

2. Practice with Hands-On Labs and Tools: Gain practical experience with common cybersecurity tools and platforms. Participate in online labs, CTFs (Capture The Flag competitions), or set up your own home lab to practice your skills in a controlled environment.

3. Stay Updated on Latest Developments: Cybersecurity is a rapidly evolving field. Stay informed about the latest security threats, vulnerabilities, and technologies by following industry blogs, attending webinars, and participating in forums and discussions.

4. Prepare Examples from Your Experience: Reflect on your past work or projects and be ready to discuss them. Think about the challenges you encountered, how you addressed them, and the results of your efforts. Be specific about the tools and methodologies you used.

5. Review the Job Description: Understand the specific requirements of the role you're applying for. Tailor your preparation to focus on the areas that are most relevant to the job description, such as specific security tools, programming languages, or compliance standards.

6. Practice Problem-Solving: Many technical interviews involve problem-solving exercises. Practice thinking through problems methodically, explaining your thought process as you go. Familiarize yourself with common types of cybersecurity puzzles and challenges.

7. Engage in Mock Interviews: Practice answering technical questions in a mock interview setting. This can help you refine your responses, improve your communication skills, and reduce interview anxiety.

# BEHAVIORAL INTERVIEWS: DEMONSTRATING YOUR SOFT SKILLS AND FIT

Behavioral interviews play a crucial role in the cybersecurity job hiring process by focusing on how you've handled various situations in the past to predict your future behavior and compatibility with the company's culture. These interviews aim to assess your soft skills, such as communication, teamwork, leadership, and problem-solving, which are as vital as technical skills in a cybersecurity context. Here's how to effectively prepare for and navigate behavioral interviews.

## Understanding Behavioral Interviews

Behavioral interviews delve into your past experiences, asking you to provide specific examples that demonstrate your soft skills. Interviewers are looking for insights into your working style, how you interact with others, your decision-making process, and how you overcome challenges. Common themes include teamwork, conflict resolution, time management, adaptability, and initiative.

## Preparing for Behavioral Interviews

1. Reflect on Your Experiences: Start by listing significant achievements and challenges in your career. Think about times when you demonstrated leadership, solved a complex problem, worked under pressure, or navigated a conflict within a team.

2. Use the STAR Method: Structure your responses using the Situation, Task, Action, Result (STAR) method. Describe the situation, outline the task at hand, detail the specific actions you took, and conclude with the results of those actions. This method helps keep your answers clear and compelling.

3. Identify Relevant Soft Skills: Match your experiences to the soft skills that are most relevant to the role you're applying for. Cybersecurity roles may particularly value skills like critical thinking,

effective communication with non-technical stakeholders, resilience in the face of challenges, and collaborative problem-solving.

4. Practice Your Responses: Rehearse your answers to common behavioral questions. Practicing out loud can help you refine your storytelling and ensure your examples effectively highlight your skills. Consider practicing with a friend or mentor who can provide feedback.

## During the Interview

1. Listen Carefully: Pay close attention to the question being asked to ensure your answer is relevant and addresses what the interviewer is seeking. Don't hesitate to ask for clarification if needed.

2. Be Authentic: Genuine responses will always make a stronger impression than rehearsed answers. While it's important to prepare, ensure your responses reflect your true experiences and personality.

3. Show Enthusiasm: Demonstrating passion for your work and eagerness to tackle new challenges can significantly enhance your appeal as a candidate. Let your enthusiasm for cybersecurity and problem-solving shine through in your answers.

4. Highlight Learning and Growth: When discussing challenges or failures, emphasize what you learned from the experience and how it contributed to your professional growth. This shows resilience and a commitment to continuous improvement.

5. Tailor Examples to the Company: Whenever possible, relate your examples to the potential challenges and situations you might face at the company you're interviewing with. Researching the company's values, culture, and current cybersecurity challenges can help you tailor your responses.

# Mastering Technical Interview Questions: How to Approach Them

Technical interviews are a critical stage in the cybersecurity job application process, designed to assess your technical knowledge, problem-solving ability, and suitability for the specific technical demands of the role. The way you approach these questions can significantly impact your performance. Here's a comprehensive guide on how to navigate and excel in answering technical interview questions.

## Understanding Technical Interview Questions

Technical interview questions in cybersecurity can range from foundational knowledge queries about networking and security principles to complex problem-solving scenarios involving threat analysis, system vulnerabilities, or cryptographic techniques. The questions may also probe your practical experience with tools, technologies, and methodologies relevant to the role.

## Strategies for Approaching Technical Questions

### 1. Clarify the Question:

Listen Carefully: Ensure you fully understand the question being asked. Pay attention to specifics that may hint at what the interviewer is looking to assess.

Ask for Clarification: If a question is unclear or broad, don't hesitate to ask for more details. Clarifying questions can help narrow down the focus and demonstrate your analytical approach.

### 2. Structure Your Response:

Think Aloud: One effective strategy is to think aloud as you structure your response. This not only buys you time to organize your thoughts but also allows the interviewer to follow your thought process, showcasing your analytical skills.

Use Frameworks: Where applicable, employ frameworks or methodologies (like the OSI model for networking questions or the CIA triad for security principles) to structure your answer logically.

### 3. Draw on Your Experience:

Practical Examples: Whenever possible, relate the question to real-world experiences or projects you've worked on. This not only provides evidence of your practical skills but also makes your response more engaging and credible.

Problem-Solving Scenarios: For problem-solving questions, walk the interviewer through your approach step by step, highlighting how you would apply your technical knowledge to address the scenario.

### 4. Focus on Fundamentals:

Solid Foundation: Ensure you have a solid grasp of cybersecurity fundamentals. Many technical questions are designed to assess your understanding of core concepts, even if they initially appear complex.

Continuous Learning: Demonstrate your commitment to staying updated with the latest developments in the field. Mention any recent articles, research, or training you've engaged with that's relevant to the question.

### 5. Communicate Limitations:

Honesty: If you don't know the answer to a question, it's better to be honest rather than guess. You can express your eagerness to learn or how you would go about finding the solution.

Partial Answers: If you partially know the answer, explain what you do know. This can sometimes be enough to satisfy the interviewer or provide a basis for discussion.

### Tips for Practicing Technical Questions

1. Review Common Questions: Research and practice answers to common technical interview questions in cybersecurity. This can include topics like encryption standards, network protocols, security frameworks, and common vulnerabilities.

2. Hands-On Practice: Engage in practical exercises, labs, and simulation platforms to reinforce your technical skills. This hands-on experience can provide vivid examples to draw upon during your interview.

3. Study Deeply: Go beyond surface-level understanding, especially for areas critical to the role you're applying for. Deep knowledge allows you to answer more confidently and tackle complex questions effectively.

4. Mock Interviews: Participate in mock interviews focusing on technical questions. This can help you refine your answering strategy, improve your communication of complex concepts, and reduce interview anxiety.

## SCENARIO-BASED QUESTIONS: APPLYING KNOWLEDGE TO REAL-WORLD SITUATIONS

Scenario-based questions are a staple of the cybersecurity interview process, designed to evaluate how you apply your technical knowledge and problem-solving skills to real-world situations. These questions simulate practical challenges you might face on the job, offering insight into your approach to identifying, analyzing, and mitigating cybersecurity threats and vulnerabilities. Understanding how to effectively tackle these questions can significantly boost your interview performance.

### Understanding Scenario-Based Questions

Scenario-based questions in cybersecurity interviews typically present a hypothetical situation related to security incidents, system vulnerabilities, threat assessments, or ethical dilemmas. The aim is to assess your critical thinking, decision-making, and technical application skills under conditions that mimic actual job challenges.

**Strategies for Tackling Scenario-Based Questions**

1. Clarify the Scenario:

Understand the Details: Ensure you grasp the key elements of the scenario by listening carefully. It's important to catch specific details that might influence your response.

Ask Clarifying Questions: If any aspect of the scenario is unclear, don't hesitate to ask for more information. This demonstrates your thoroughness and attention to detail.

2. Break Down the Problem:

Identify Key Issues: Start by identifying the core problems or security concerns presented in the scenario. Outline these issues to structure your response around addressing them.

Prioritize Actions: Determine which issues need immediate attention and which can be addressed later. Prioritization is crucial in cybersecurity response efforts.

3. Apply Methodical Problem-Solving:

Employ Frameworks: Where applicable, use cybersecurity frameworks or methodologies to guide your response. For instance, you might apply the incident response phases (preparation, identification, containment, eradication, recovery, lessons learned) to organize your strategy.

Leverage Technical Knowledge: Draw on your technical expertise to propose specific tools, techniques, or practices that would effectively address the situation. Be detailed about why and how you would use these resources.

4. Discuss the Impact:

Consider Consequences: Discuss the potential consequences of the scenario if not properly addressed, and how your actions would mitigate those risks. This shows an understanding of the broader implications of cybersecurity issues.

Highlight Preventative Measures: Beyond immediate response, mention any preventative measures or policy changes that could reduce future risk. This demonstrates forward-thinking and a comprehensive approach to security.

5. Communicate Effectively:

Articulate Your Thought Process: Clearly explain your reasoning as you walk through your response. This helps interviewers follow your thought process and assess your problem-solving skills.

Stay Concise and Relevant: While detail is important, aim to keep your response focused and avoid unnecessary tangents. Efficiency in communication is key, especially in crisis situations.

## Preparing for Scenario-Based Questions

1. Review Common Scenarios: Familiarize yourself with common types of cybersecurity scenarios, such as data breaches, phishing attacks, ransomware incidents, and DDoS attacks. Understanding how to respond to these can prepare you for a range of questions.

2. Practice with Real-World Examples: Reflect on any real-world incidents you've dealt with in past roles or studied. Consider how you would apply those experiences to the scenarios you might face in the interview.

3. Stay Informed: Keep up-to-date with recent cybersecurity incidents and trends. This can provide timely, relevant examples to reference in your responses and demonstrate your engagement with the field.

4. Engage in Thought Experiments: Regularly challenge yourself with hypothetical scenarios. Think through how you would respond, what tools you would use, and the potential challenges you would face. This practice can sharpen your problem-solving skills and prepare you for unexpected questions.

# DEMONSTRATING LEADERSHIP AND CONFLICT RESOLUTION SKILLS

In the dynamic and often high-pressure environment of cybersecurity, leadership and conflict resolution skills are invaluable. Cybersecurity professionals are frequently called upon to lead teams, manage projects, and navigate conflicts that may arise due to the high-stakes nature of security work. Excelling in these areas can set you apart in your career and during the interview process for cybersecurity roles. Here's how to effectively demonstrate these crucial skills during your job interview.

## Understanding Leadership in Cybersecurity

Leadership in cybersecurity involves more than just managing people. It encompasses setting a vision for security practices, inspiring a culture of security awareness, making strategic decisions under pressure, and guiding teams through complex security challenges. Effective leadership ensures that cybersecurity measures align with the organization's goals and that teams are motivated and equipped to protect the organization's digital assets.

## Demonstrating Leadership Skills

1. Share Specific Examples: Prepare stories from your past experiences where you took the lead on cybersecurity projects or initiatives. Highlight situations where you identified a security risk, proposed a solution, and led the implementation to safeguard the

organization.

2. Highlight Strategic Decision-Making: Discuss instances where you made critical decisions that impacted your organization's security posture. Explain the rationale behind your decisions, the alternatives considered, and the outcomes achieved.

3. Emphasize Team Building and Motivation: Talk about how you've built and maintained effective cybersecurity teams. Include examples of how you've mentored team members, fostered a collaborative environment, and motivated your team to achieve their best.

4. Mention Cross-Functional Collaboration: Leadership often involves working with other departments to achieve security objectives. Share experiences where you collaborated with non-security departments to integrate security into broader organizational processes.

### Understanding Conflict Resolution in Cybersecurity

Conflict resolution skills are crucial in cybersecurity, where differing opinions on risk management, resource allocation, and security priorities can lead to conflicts. Being able to navigate these disagreements constructively is key to maintaining a strong security posture and a cohesive team.

### Demonstrating Conflict Resolution Skills

1. Prepare Real-Life Scenarios: Think of times when you faced conflicts related to cybersecurity, whether it was with team members, management, or other departments. Be ready to discuss these scenarios, focusing on the conflict's nature, your approach to resolution, and the outcome.

2. Describe Your Approach to Resolution: Detail your method for resolving conflicts, which may include active listening, empathy, clear

communication, and seeking win-win solutions. Emphasize your ability to stay calm under pressure and maintain a focus on the organization's overarching security goals.

3. Highlight the Importance of Communication: Effective conflict resolution is often grounded in clear communication. Describe how you communicate security concerns and solutions to various stakeholders to prevent misunderstandings and conflicts.

4. Discuss Learning and Improvement: Conflicts can be learning opportunities. Share how past conflicts have led to improvements in security processes, policies, or team dynamics. This demonstrates your ability to turn challenges into positive outcomes.

## PREPARING FOR LEADERSHIP AND CONFLICT RESOLUTION QUESTIONS

1. Reflect on Your Experiences: Before the interview, spend time reflecting on your leadership experiences and times you've successfully resolved conflicts. This reflection will help you quickly recall relevant examples during the interview.

2. Use the STAR Method: Structure your responses using the Situation, Task, Action, Result format to ensure they are clear and concise. This method is particularly effective for communicating complex leadership and conflict resolution scenarios.

3. Practice Articulating Your Stories: Rehearse telling your leadership and conflict resolution stories out loud. This practice can help you refine how you present your experiences, ensuring you highlight your skills effectively.

# NEGOTIATING JOB OFFERS IN THE CYBERSECURITY FIELD

Navigating the negotiation phase of a cybersecurity job offer is a critical step in your career progression. Given the high demand for skilled cybersecurity professionals, you often have leverage to negotiate not just salary but also benefits, work-life balance, professional development opportunities, and other terms of employment. Here's a guide to effectively negotiating job offers in the cybersecurity field.

## Understanding Your Worth

1. Research Industry Standards: Before entering negotiations, research the typical salary range and benefits for the role you're being offered, considering factors like your experience, certifications, the job's location, and the size of the organization. Websites like Glassdoor, PayScale, and the Bureau of Labor Statistics can provide valuable benchmarks.

2. Evaluate Your Unique Value: Reflect on what makes you a particularly valuable candidate for the position. This could be specialized certifications, specific technical expertise, successful project leadership, or experience in a niche area of cybersecurity. Being able to articulate this unique value can strengthen your negotiating position.

## Preparing for Negotiation

1. Prioritize Your Terms: Determine what aspects of the offer are most important to you. While salary is a significant factor, other elements like flexible working hours, remote work options, professional development opportunities, or additional vacation time can also be critical to your job satisfaction and should be considered in your negotiations.

2. Practice Your Approach: Rehearse how you'll present your counteroffer and responses to possible employer objections. Being

prepared will help you communicate more confidently and effectively.

**Navigating the Negotiation Process**

1. Express Enthusiasm: Start by expressing your excitement about the role and your eagerness to contribute to the organization. This sets a positive tone for the negotiation.

2. Present Your Case Clearly: Use the research and preparation you've done to present a reasoned case for your salary expectations and other terms. Be specific about why you believe these terms are justified based on your skills, experience, and the value you bring to the team.

3. Be Open to Counteroffers: Negotiations are a two-way process. Listen to the employer's counteroffers and be prepared to adjust your expectations if necessary. If the salary is non-negotiable, consider focusing on other aspects of the package, like bonuses, benefits, or work flexibility.

4. Discuss Professional Development: Cybersecurity is an evolving field, and ongoing learning is essential. Negotiate for opportunities like conference attendance, training courses, or certification sponsorships that can help you stay at the cutting edge of the industry.

5. Know When to Wrap Up: Once you reach an agreement that satisfies both parties, or it becomes clear that the employer's best offer doesn't meet your needs or expectations, be prepared to make a decision. If you accept the offer, do so with enthusiasm. If you must decline, do it graciously, keeping the door open for future opportunities.

**Finalizing the Offer**

1. Get It in Writing: Once you've verbally agreed on the terms, ask for the offer to be sent to you in writing. This document should include all aspects of your compensation package, including salary,

benefits, work schedule, and any agreed-upon conditions related to professional development.

2. Review Carefully: Review the written offer carefully to ensure it matches what was agreed upon during negotiations. If everything is in order, you can sign the offer letter and begin preparing for your new role.

# CONTINUOUS LEARNING AND CAREER DEVELOPMENT IN CYBERSECURITY

The cybersecurity landscape is perpetually evolving, with new technologies, threats, and methodologies emerging at a rapid pace. This constant change demands that professionals in the field commit to ongoing learning and career development to stay effective and relevant. Embracing continuous learning not only enhances your skill set but also opens up new career opportunities and pathways for advancement. Here's how to approach continuous learning and career development in cybersecurity.

## Embracing a Mindset of Continuous Learning

Cultivating Curiosity: Stay curious about new developments in cybersecurity. This mindset will drive you to seek out learning opportunities and stay engaged with the ever-changing field.

Setting Personal Learning Goals: Identify specific areas within cybersecurity that you want to explore or deepen your expertise in. Setting goals can help focus your learning efforts and measure progress.

## Strategies for Continuous Learning

1. Formal Education and Training Programs: Consider pursuing further formal education such as cybersecurity degrees, graduate

certificates, or specialized training programs. Many institutions offer online learning options, making it easier to fit education into your schedule.

2. Professional Certifications: Earning certifications is a powerful way to validate your skills and knowledge. Certifications such as CISSP, CISM, CEH, or CompTIA Security+ are highly regarded in the industry and often lead to new opportunities and career growth.

3. Online Learning Platforms: Platforms like Coursera, Udemy, and Cybrary offer a wide range of courses covering various cybersecurity topics. These platforms are an excellent resource for learning at your own pace.

4. Industry Conferences and Workshops: Attend cybersecurity conferences, workshops, and webinars. These events are great for learning about the latest trends, networking with peers, and sometimes offer hands-on training sessions.

5. Reading and Research: Stay informed by reading industry publications, blogs, and research papers. Follow thought leaders on social media and participate in online forums and communities.

6. Personal Projects and Lab Work: Hands-on experience is invaluable. Set up a home lab to experiment with new tools and technologies, or work on personal projects related to areas of cybersecurity that interest you.

## Career Development in Cybersecurity

Networking: Build and maintain a professional network within the cybersecurity community. Networking can lead to mentorship opportunities, job offers, and valuable insights into career progression.

Mentorship: Seek out mentors who can provide guidance, advice, and feedback on your career path. Being a mentor to others can also enhance your leadership skills and deepen your own understanding of cybersecurity topics.

Specialization: Consider specializing in a niche area of cybersecurity. Specialization can make you highly sought after for expert roles in areas like penetration testing, cyber law, incident response, or secure software development.

Leadership and Management Skills: As you progress in your career, developing leadership and management skills becomes increasingly important. Look for opportunities to lead projects, manage teams, or contribute to strategic planning within your organization.

Contribute to the Community: Sharing your knowledge and experiences by writing blog posts, speaking at conferences, or volunteering for cybersecurity awareness initiatives can raise your profile in the field and contribute to the community.

# CYBERSECURITY INTERVIEW QUESTIONS

After your standout cybersecurity resume and cover letter have successfully secured an interview, it's time to gear up for the Cybersecurity interview phase. The interview dynamics for cybersecurity roles can differ widely based on the organization and the specific position you're applying for.

Typically, the interview journey might start with an initial discussion with the Hiring Manager, which could lead to a more formal interview involving the Hiring Manager and possibly a group of team members.

During the interview stages, expect to navigate through a variety of technical and situational questions. These inquiries aim to assess both your cybersecurity expertise and your compatibility with the organizational culture.

To aid in your preparation, we've gathered a selection of frequent interview questions along with answers tailored for cybersecurity positions, ensuring you're well-prepared for the breadth of topics that may be covered.

## GENERAL SKILLS-BASED CYBERSECURITY INTERVIEW QUESTIONS

During a cybersecurity job interview, anticipate that a significant portion of the discussion will revolve around your understanding of cybersecurity fundamentals, your practical experience with various standard operations, and your capability to stay abreast of an ever-evolving industry.

**Question: Can you explain what a Brute Force Attack is and**

**how to mitigate it?**

A Brute Force Attack is an attempt to crack encrypted data, such as passwords, by systematically checking all possible keys or passwords until the correct one is found. These attacks often employ automated tools to try a wide array of combinations. To counteract these types of attacks, one could implement policies requiring robust password criteria, such as complexity and length, ensuring no default passwords are in use within the organization. Additionally, adopting multi-factor authentication and limiting the number of unsuccessful login attempts are effective preventive measures.

**Question: How do black hat hackers differ from white hat hackers?**

Black hat hackers are individuals who exploit computer systems or networks without authorization, using methods like brute force attacks, with malicious intent, such as theft of data or causing disruption. In contrast, white hat hackers employ similar techniques but with the lawful intention of identifying and fixing security vulnerabilities to safeguard data against such malicious threats. Their goal is to enhance an organization's security posture.

1. **What is cryptography?**
   - Cryptography is the practice and study of techniques for securing communication and data in the presence of adversaries through encryption and related methods.
2. **How do you define the differences between symmetric and asymmetric encryption?**
   - Symmetric encryption uses the same key for encryption and decryption, while asymmetric encryption uses a pair of keys (public and private) where one encrypts and the other decrypts.
3. **How do you define the differences between IDS and IPS?**
   - An Intrusion Detection System (IDS) monitors network traffic for suspicious activity and issues alerts,

whereas an Intrusion Prevention System (IPS) actively blocks potential threats based on detected suspicious activities.

4. **What is the CIA triad?**
   - The CIA triad stands for Confidentiality, Integrity, and Availability, three key principles guiding information security policies and practices.

5. **How do you define the differences between encoding, encryption, and hashing?**
   - Encoding is the process of converting data into a different format using a scheme. Encryption is the process of converting data into a secure format that cannot be read without a key. Hashing is the process of converting data into a fixed-size string of characters, which acts as a fingerprint of the data.

6. **Do you have experience with Traceroute?**
   - Yes, Traceroute is a network diagnostic tool used to track the pathway taken by a packet on an IP network from source to destination, revealing the route and measuring transit delays.

7. **What steps would you take to prevent an XSS attack?**
   - To prevent an XSS (Cross-Site Scripting) attack, validate and sanitize all user input, encode data on output, implement Content Security Policy (CSP), and use secure frameworks that automatically escape XSS vulnerabilities.

8. **What would be your process to set up a firewall?**
   - Setting up a firewall involves defining and implementing a set of rules that specify allowed and denied traffic, configuring the firewall according to the network's security requirements, regularly updating its firmware, and monitoring firewall logs for suspicious activity.

9. **What is a Virtual Private Network (VPN)?**
   - A VPN is a service that creates a secure, encrypted connection over a less secure network, such as the internet, to provide privacy and anonymity for data transmission.

10. **What is cross-site scripting?**
    - Cross-site scripting (XSS) is a web security vulnerability that allows attackers to inject malicious

scripts into content from otherwise trusted websites, potentially compromising the confidentiality and integrity of user sessions.

**How frequently do you perform Patch management?**

Patch management is conducted on a regular basis, aligning with the release schedules of vendors, but at least monthly to ensure systems are safeguarded against new vulnerabilities.

**What is your process to prevent identity theft?**

Preventing identity theft involves implementing stringent password policies, enabling multi-factor authentication, conducting regular security awareness training, encrypting sensitive information, and monitoring financial and personal data for unauthorized access.

**Please take us through your understanding of risk, vulnerability, and threat within a network?**

- **Risk** is the potential for loss or harm to a system or organization due to a vulnerability being exploited by a threat.
- **Vulnerability** is a weakness or flaw in a system that can be exploited by a threat to cause harm.
- **Threat** is any circumstance or event with the potential to cause harm to a system or organization by exploiting a vulnerability.

**What steps would you take to prevent an MITM attack?**

To prevent MITM attacks, I would enforce the use of strong encryption for data in transit, deploy HTTPS across all web services, implement certificate pinning where appropriate, and educate users on the importance of secure connections.

**What is the difference between a threat, a vulnerability, and a risk?**

- **Threat:** An action or event that might compromise security.
- **Vulnerability:** A weakness that can be exploited by a threat to breach security.

- **Risk:** The potential impact or damage that can occur when a threat exploits a vulnerability.

## Why is DNS monitoring important?

DNS monitoring is crucial for identifying and mitigating malicious activities like DNS hijacking, amplification attacks, and cache poisoning, thereby maintaining the integrity and availability of domain resolution services.

## What is two-factor authentication?

Two-factor authentication (2FA) is a security process in which users provide two different authentication factors to verify themselves. This method adds an additional layer of security to the authentication process, making it harder for attackers to gain access to a person's devices or online accounts.

## How would you define Secure Sockets Layer (SSL)?

Secure Sockets Layer (SSL) is a standard security protocol for establishing encrypted links between a web server and a browser, ensuring that all data transmitted remains private and integral.

## TECHNICAL CYBERSECURITY INTERVIEW QUESTIONS

Positions in cybersecurity are notably technical. Once your interviewer has assessed your foundational knowledge of cybersecurity principles, they're likely to delve into more intricate subjects and technical duties to verify your combination of practical experience and technical know-how.

## Can you name the layers of the OSI model?

Answer: The OSI (Open Systems Interconnection) model comprises seven distinct layers:

- Physical Layer
- Data Link Layer
- Network Layer
- Transport Layer
- Session Layer
- Presentation Layer
- Application Layer

## How would you go about securing a server?

In the context of cybersecurity positions, interviewers will be interested in your practical experience with safeguarding web servers. A recommended initial action in your answer would be to implement secure password practices for administrative and root accounts, followed by disabling remote access for default admin and root accounts. The concluding action would involve establishing a firewall to scrutinize and manage network traffic, thereby safeguarding the system against potential threats like malware, viruses, or worms.

## How would you identify a compromised system?

To identify a compromised system, I would monitor for unusual activity that deviates from normal operations. This includes unexpected system reboots, slow system performance, unexplained network traffic, unusual outbound communication, ransomware messages, or unfamiliar programs running at startup. Implementing intrusion detection systems (IDS) and using security information and event management (SIEM) tools can aid in detecting anomalies. Regularly auditing logs for unauthorized access attempts and ensuring antivirus and endpoint detection and response (EDR) solutions are up to date are critical steps in early identification of compromised systems.

## Imagine you have to both compress and encrypt data during a transmission. Which would you do first?

Compression should be performed before encryption for a couple of reasons. Firstly, encryption randomizes data, which can significantly reduce the effectiveness of compression. Secondly, compressing data after encryption is practically ineffective since encrypted data shows very high entropy (randomness). By compressing first, you ensure that the data is minimized in size, which then can be encrypted more efficiently for secure transmission.

**What is your approach to defend against a cross-site scripting attack?**

To defend against cross-site scripting (XSS) attacks, I would implement content security policies (CSP) to specify which dynamic resources are allowed to load. Ensuring that user input is sanitized, validated, and encoded before being displayed on web pages is crucial. Utilizing secure frameworks that automatically escape XSS by design and employing HTTP-only and Secure flags in cookies to prevent script access to cookies are also effective strategies.

**What are the differences between cybersecurity in the cloud and on-premises?**

Cybersecurity in the cloud differs from on-premises mainly in the shared responsibility model. In the cloud, security is shared between the cloud service provider, responsible for securing the infrastructure, and the customer, who must secure their data and applications. Cloud environments often offer scalability, automation, and integration with advanced security services. On-premises environments give organizations full control over their security measures but require significant investment in hardware, software, and personnel.

**What is the difference between symmetric and asymmetric encryption?**

Symmetric encryption uses the same key for both encryption and decryption, making it fast and suitable for encrypting large volumes of data. However, key distribution poses a challenge. Asymmetric encryption, or public-key cryptography, uses a pair of keys – a public key for encryption and a private key for decryption. This solves the key distribution problem but is more computationally intensive, making it less efficient for encrypting large amounts of data.

**How do you define data leakage and its types?**

Data leakage refers to the unauthorized transmission of data from within an organization to an external destination or recipient. The types of data leakage can include accidental sharing of sensitive information via emails, unauthorized data transfers to external storage devices, exposure of data through misconfigured services, or deliberate theft of confidential information by insiders or through cyberattacks.

**Can you please define the process of salting?**

Salting is a security measure used in password hashing to defend against dictionary attacks and rainbow table attacks. It involves adding a unique, random string of characters, known as a salt, to each password before it is hashed. The salted password is then hashed, and both the salt and the hashed password are stored. Since the salt is unique for each password, it ensures that identical passwords will have different hashes, greatly increasing the difficulty for an attacker to crack the passwords.

**What is the difference between UDP and TCP?**

TCP (Transmission Control Protocol) is a connection-oriented protocol that ensures reliable, ordered delivery of data packets over the network. It establishes a connection before transmitting data and confirms receipt of packets. UDP (User Datagram Protocol) is a connectionless protocol that sends packets without establishing a connection or guaranteeing delivery. UDP is faster but less reliable than TCP and is used where speed is critical and occasional data loss is acceptable, such as streaming audio or video.

**What is the application of address resolution protocol (ARP)?**

The Address Resolution Protocol (ARP) is used to map an IP address to its corresponding physical MAC (Media Access Control) address in a local area network (LAN). This is necessary for communication between devices on the same network segment when data packets need to be sent at the link layer. ARP is essential for IPv4 networking, enabling devices to discover the MAC address of another device with which they wish to communicate.

## What is a black box penetration test?

A black box penetration test is a type of security assessment where the tester is given no prior knowledge of the target system or network. This approach simulates an attack by an external threat actor who has no inside information, allowing organizations to understand how an attacker could exploit their systems from the outside. It focuses on identifying vulnerabilities that could be discovered and exploited without internal access.

## What are the default ports for HTTP and for HTTPS?

The default port for HTTP (HyperText Transfer Protocol) is port 80. This is the standard port used by web browsers and servers for transmitting web pages and other content over an unsecured connection. For HTTPS (HTTP Secure), the default port is 443. HTTPS is used for secure communications over a computer network, with data encrypted for security, making it widely used for transactional data and personal information to ensure privacy and confidentiality.

## What is a polymorphic virus?

A polymorphic virus is a type of malware that has the ability to change or mutate its underlying code without changing its basic functions or features. This mutation occurs every time it infects a new system, making it extremely difficult for traditional antivirus software to detect using signature-based methods. The polymorphic nature allows the virus to avoid detection by creating a unique instance of itself in each infection, necessitating more advanced or behavior-based detection techniques to protect against it.

**What is a null session?**

A null session is a type of network connection where a client connects to a server without providing any credentials. This anonymous connection is allowed through the inter-process communication share (IPC$) to enable certain types of data exchanges, typically for administrative tasks. Null sessions can be exploited by attackers to anonymously enumerate and gather sensitive information about network resources, users, and groups, making it a significant security concern. Therefore, securing and limiting null session connections is crucial in network security management.

**What is the difference between spear phishing and phishing?**

Phishing and spear phishing are both forms of cyberattacks that aim to trick individuals into revealing sensitive information, such as passwords or credit card numbers. The key difference lies in their approach and specificity. Phishing attacks are broad and untargeted, often sent to large numbers of users with the hope that some will be deceived. These attacks might take the form of generic emails purporting to be from reputable organizations, requesting personal information or urging the recipient to click on malicious links. Spear phishing, on the other hand, is highly targeted. Attackers spend time researching their victims to create personalized messages, often impersonating a trusted colleague, friend, or organization. This method significantly increases the likelihood that the recipient will trust the content and act on the requests made in the message.

**What is the term for the situation when a user is attacked by directing them to what they think is a legitimate site, but it is actually a scam site?**

The situation described is known as "pharming." Pharming involves redirecting a user from a legitimate website to a fraudulent one without their knowledge or consent. This is typically achieved through DNS hijacking or poisoning, where the attacker alters the DNS entry of a website on a DNS server or on the user's computer, so that traffic intended for a specific site is sent to a malicious one instead. Unlike phishing, which relies on tricking users into clicking a link, pharming can be more insidious, as users may enter the correct URL and still end up on the scam site.

## What's the difference between logging and auditing?

Logging and auditing are both processes used to record events and changes within systems, but they serve different purposes. Logging is the act of recording specific events or actions, such as user logins, system errors, or transactions, typically in real-time. Logs provide a detailed, timestamped record of what has occurred on a system, which is crucial for troubleshooting, performance monitoring, and detecting anomalous behavior. Auditing, on the other hand, is a more formal and systematic process of reviewing and examining logs, records, and operations within a system or organization to ensure compliance with policies, standards, and regulations. Auditing involves analyzing the logged information to verify the integrity and security of systems, assess risk management practices, and ensure accountability.

## Explain why you would do a vulnerability assessment instead of a penetration test.

A vulnerability assessment is a comprehensive examination of an organization's systems and networks to identify and quantify security vulnerabilities. Its primary goal is to catalog potential threats and provide remediation advice without actively exploiting the vulnerabilities. This approach is valuable for organizations that want a broad understanding of their security posture and a prioritized list of vulnerabilities to address. On the other hand, a penetration test (pentest) involves simulating a cyberattack to exploit vulnerabilities actively. While pentests provide insight into how an attacker could breach a system and the potential impact, they are more intrusive and resource-intensive. Organizations might choose a vulnerability assessment over a pentest when they seek a less aggressive approach to identify vulnerabilities, especially when they are in the early stages of building a security program or are more interested in a comprehensive inventory of potential vulnerabilities rather than testing their defenses against an attack.

## What kind of cookie would a spyware attack typically use?

A spyware attack would typically use a tracking cookie. Tracking cookies are designed to monitor and record users' online activities, preferences, and personally identifiable information as they navigate through different websites. While tracking cookies are widely used in marketing to personalize user experiences and targeted advertising, they can be exploited by spyware to gather data without the user's consent, compromising privacy. Spyware uses these cookies to collect a wide range of information, which can include browsing habits, login credentials, and other sensitive data that can be used for malicious purposes, such as identity theft or targeted phishing attacks.

## What is the difference between a virus and a worm?

The primary distinction between a virus and a worm lies in their method of propagation. A virus is a type of malware that attaches itself to legitimate software and requires some form of user interaction, such as executing a file or opening an infected email attachment, to activate and replicate. Once activated, it can corrupt files, steal data, or damage the system's functionality. A worm, on the other hand, is a self-replicating malware that does not require attachment to a separate program or user interaction to spread. Worms exploit vulnerabilities in operating systems or other software to propagate automatically across networks. This autonomous propagation allows worms to spread more rapidly and widely than viruses, potentially leading to widespread disruption and damage.

## How do you prevent outdated software from being exploited?

Preventing outdated software from being exploited involves implementing a comprehensive patch management strategy. This strategy should include regularly updating all software and systems with the latest security patches and updates released by vendors. It's crucial to inventory all software and hardware assets to ensure none are overlooked during the update process. Automated patch management tools can assist in identifying and applying necessary updates efficiently. Additionally, using vulnerability scanning tools to identify outdated software and known vulnerabilities can help prioritize updates. Employing a layered security approach, including firewalls, antivirus solutions, and intrusion detection systems, can also mitigate the risk of exploitation in case any outdated software remains temporarily unpatched.

**Which attacks involve the use of previously captured network traffic?**

Attacks involving the use of previously captured network traffic are commonly referred to as replay attacks. In a replay attack, an attacker intercepts and records legitimate traffic, such as authentication tokens, session cookies, or digital signatures, and then retransmits it to the server or target device. The goal is to fool the system into granting access or performing an unauthorized transaction as if the messages originated from the legitimate user. This type of attack exploits the lack of proper session management and timestamping in the communication protocol, allowing the attacker to reuse or "replay" captured data to achieve unauthorized access or initiate fraudulent transactions.

**What is the term for a situation when somebody is forced to reveal cryptographic secrets through physical threats?**

The term for a situation when somebody is forced to reveal cryptographic secrets through physical threats is known as "rubber-hose cryptanalysis" or more informally, "rubber-hosing." This term humorously suggests that coercion, or other forms of duress could be used to compel an individual to divulge cryptographic keys, passwords, or other sensitive information necessary to decrypt data. Unlike technical or mathematical methods of breaking encryption, rubber-hose cryptanalysis relies on physical or psychological pressure to bypass cryptographic security measures.

**What cybersecurity tool would you use to quickly search through logs with regular expression?**

To quickly search through logs with regular expressions, I would use a log management tool that supports regular expression (regex) searching, such as Splunk or Elasticsearch with Kibana. These tools are designed for collecting, analyzing, and visualizing log data from various sources in real-time, offering powerful search capabilities that include the use of regular expressions. Regular expressions allow for pattern matching, which can be incredibly useful for identifying specific events, anomalies, or trends within large volumes of log data. By leveraging regex searches in tools like Splunk or Elasticsearch, cybersecurity professionals can efficiently sift through logs to detect potential security incidents or troubleshoot issues.

**You find out an employee has been downloading unrelated work content. What actions would you take?**

Upon discovering that an employee engaged in downloading unrelated work content, my initial step would be to engage in a direct conversation with them to understand their motives. Should it appear to be an oversight or misunderstanding on their part, I would issue a formal warning and require them to acknowledge in writing their understanding of the rules and potential repercussions of such actions in the future. Conversely, if the act was found to be deliberate with harmful intent, immediate termination of their employment would be considered necessary."

**You discover an employee sharing sensitive data on social media.**

Upon discovering sensitive information being shared by an employee on social media, my priority would be to assess the nature and sensitivity of the shared data. If the shared data is harmless and does not compromise any company security, a reminder of our company's privacy policies might suffice. However, if the data shared poses a risk of a security breach, it would necessitate more stringent measures. Documentation of all proceedings is crucial in both scenarios, serving as protection in potential legal proceedings and as a preventive measure against future occurrences."

**If you were to engage in unauthorized data retrieval from a company, how would you proceed?**

"Extracting data from a company without authorization typically involves exploiting existing security weaknesses. Hackers frequently scan for systems with unaddressed vulnerabilities to exploit these gaps. Gaining entry allows them to either exfiltrate sensitive information directly or install malware for long-term access, posing significant risks to the company's data integrity."

**What risks come with public Wi-Fi?**

Using public Wi-Fi introduces several risks, primarily due to the lack of secure encryption, making it easier for malicious actors to intercept data transmitted over the network. Key risks include man-in-the-middle (MITM) attacks, where an attacker intercepts communication between two parties to steal or manipulate data. Public Wi-Fi can also be a breeding ground for distributing malware, where attackers compromise the network to inject malware into connected devices. Additionally, unsecured Wi-Fi networks can lead to identity theft if personal or financial information is intercepted. Network spoofing is another risk, where attackers set up fake Wi-Fi access points that mimic legitimate ones to deceive users into connecting.

**What is the main difference between RSA and Diffie-Hellman?**

The main difference between RSA (Rivest-Shamir-Adleman) and Diffie-Hellman algorithms lies in their primary use cases. RSA is both an encryption and digital signature algorithm, which means it is used for encrypting data and securely transmitting it over the internet, as well as for authenticating the integrity and origin of a message through digital signatures. Diffie-Hellman, on the other hand, is specifically used for securely exchanging cryptographic keys over a public channel and does not directly encrypt or sign data. While RSA uses a pair of public and private keys for its operations, Diffie-Hellman allows two parties to generate a shared secret key, which can then be used for encryption and decryption.

**What is port scanning?**

Port scanning is a technique used to identify open ports and services available on a host network or system. It involves sending a message to each port, one at a time, and listening for responses to identify which ports are open and listening, which are closed, and which are filtered by a firewall. Port scanning is utilized by network administrators to verify security policies of their systems and by attackers to identify vulnerable services and potentially exploit them. Effective port scanning can reveal the services running on a system and provide insights into the system's vulnerabilities, making it a critical preliminary step in the network exploration phase of a penetration test.

**What protocols fall under TCP/IP internet layer?**

The TCP/IP Internet Layer, also known as the network layer, is responsible for packet forwarding, including routing through intermediate routers. Protocols that fall under this layer include:

- **IP (Internet Protocol):** The primary protocol in this layer, responsible for addressing and routing packets of data so that they can travel across networks and arrive at the correct destination.
- **ICMP (Internet Control Message Protocol):** Used by network devices, like routers, to send error messages and operational information indicating, for example, that a requested service is not available or a router could not be reached.
- **IGMP (Internet Group Management Protocol):** Used by IP hosts and adjacent routers on IPv4 networks to establish multicast group memberships.
- **ARP (Address Resolution Protocol):** Used to convert an IP address into a physical address, such as an Ethernet address.
- **RARP (Reverse Address Resolution Protocol):** Used to find the IP address of a host from its physical address.

These protocols work together to ensure data is transmitted efficiently across the internet and other packet-switched networks.

**Please define forward secrecy.**

Forward secrecy, also known as perfect forward secrecy (PFS), is a property of secure communication protocols in which the keys used for encrypting messages cannot be derived from any of the session keys used in future sessions. This means that even if an attacker manages to compromise the private keys of a server, they would not be able to decrypt past communications. Forward secrecy is achieved by generating unique session keys for each interaction that are not based on a static server key. This ensures that the compromise of a single session key would only affect the security of that particular session, with no impact on the confidentiality of previous or future communications.

**Please explain the difference between stream cipher and block cipher.**

Stream ciphers and block ciphers are both methods of encrypting data, but they operate differently. A stream cipher encrypts plaintext one byte or bit at a time, making it well-suited for encrypting data streams of an undefined length. It works by generating a keystream, which is then combined with the plaintext to produce ciphertext. This method is generally faster and uses less memory, making it suitable for real-time encryption and smaller devices. On the other hand, a block cipher encrypts data in fixed-size blocks (e.g., 128 or 256 bits), applying the same encryption algorithm and key on each block independently. This approach is more robust in terms of security but can be slower and more resource-intensive. Block ciphers can also operate in different modes to enhance security, including ECB, CBC, and GCM, among others.

**What is cognitive cyber security?**

Cognitive cybersecurity is an application of AI technologies, particularly machine learning and natural language processing, to automatically detect and respond to cyber threats without human intervention. It involves the creation of self-learning systems that can analyze security data at scale, understand the context, identify patterns, and make decisions to prevent or mitigate cyber attacks. Cognitive systems can adapt to new threats over time, learning from previous incidents and security research to improve their detection capabilities. This approach allows for more efficient processing of the vast amount of data generated by network devices and applications, enabling quicker response times and freeing up human security analysts to focus on more complex analysis and strategic security planning.

## Define a buffer overflow attack.

A buffer overflow attack occurs when more data is written to a buffer, a temporary data storage area, than it is designed to hold. Since buffers have a finite capacity, excess data can overflow into adjacent memory spaces, overwriting valid data or control information. Attackers exploit buffer overflow vulnerabilities to corrupt the execution stack of a software application, allowing them to execute arbitrary code or gain unauthorized access to a system. This type of attack is particularly dangerous because it can lead to the compromise of system security, data confidentiality, and integrity. Preventing buffer overflow attacks involves careful coding practices, such as bounds checking, and the use of security features like stack canaries, address space layout randomization (ASLR), and non-executable memory protections.

## What is CryptoAPI?

CryptoAPI, short for Cryptographic Application Programming Interface, is a set of programming interfaces provided by Microsoft Windows operating systems to enable developers to incorporate cryptographic functionality into their applications. It offers a range of cryptographic services, including encryption, decryption, hashing, digital signatures, and key management. CryptoAPI supports various cryptographic algorithms and protocols, allowing applications to secure sensitive data, authenticate users, and ensure the integrity and confidentiality of communications. It provides a standardized interface for interacting with cryptographic components, simplifying the implementation of secure cryptographic features in Windows-based software.

## What is an SQL Injection?

An SQL Injection (SQLi) is a type of cyber attack that exploits vulnerabilities in web applications to manipulate or extract data from a backend database using malicious SQL queries. In an SQL injection attack, an attacker injects arbitrary SQL code into input fields or parameters of a web application that interact with a database. If the application fails to properly validate or sanitize user input, the injected SQL code can be executed by the database server, leading to unauthorized access, data leakage, data manipulation, or even full database compromise. SQL injection attacks are prevalent and pose a significant threat to web applications that use dynamic SQL queries to interact with databases. Preventive measures include input validation, parameterized queries, using prepared statements, and implementing least privilege access controls.

**What are some common types of non-physical attacks?**

Non-physical attacks, also known as cyber attacks, encompass a wide range of malicious activities targeting computer systems, networks, and digital assets. Some common types of non-physical attacks include:

1. Malware: Malicious software designed to disrupt, damage, or gain unauthorized access to computer systems, including viruses, worms, trojans, ransomware, and spyware.
2. Phishing: Deceptive techniques used to trick individuals into disclosing sensitive information, such as usernames, passwords, or financial details, often through fraudulent emails, websites, or messages.
3. Denial-of-Service (DoS) and Distributed Denial-of-Service (DDoS) attacks: Attempts to overwhelm a target system or network with a flood of traffic, rendering it inaccessible to legitimate users.
4. Man-in-the-Middle (MitM) attacks: Interception and manipulation of communication between two parties to eavesdrop on or modify transmitted data without the knowledge or consent of the users.
5. Cross-Site Scripting (XSS): Injection of malicious scripts into web pages viewed by other users, allowing attackers to steal

session cookies, deface websites, or execute unauthorized actions on behalf of users.

These attacks can have severe consequences, including data breaches, financial losses, reputational damage, and disruption of business operations.

**What is a botnet?**

A botnet is a network of compromised computers, also known as bots or zombies, that are infected with malicious software and controlled remotely by a central command-and-control (C&C) infrastructure operated by an attacker. Botnets are typically created by infecting a large number of vulnerable computers with malware, such as viruses, worms, or trojans, often through phishing attacks or exploiting software vulnerabilities. Once infected, these compromised computers become part of the botnet and can be used to carry out various malicious activities, such as:

- Sending spam emails
- Launching distributed denial-of-service (DDoS) attacks
- Spreading malware or ransomware
- Harvesting sensitive information, such as login credentials or financial data
- Click fraud or ad fraud
- Mining cryptocurrencies

Botnets are a significant threat to cybersecurity because they can leverage the combined computing power of multiple compromised devices to conduct large-scale attacks with minimal effort. Detecting and mitigating botnet infections often require advanced threat detection techniques, network monitoring, and security measures such as firewalls, intrusion detection systems (IDS), and antivirus software.

**Please define system hardening.**

System hardening refers to the process of enhancing the security of a computer system or network infrastructure by reducing its attack surface and minimizing potential vulnerabilities and security risks.

The goal of system hardening is to strengthen the overall security posture of a system by implementing various security measures, configurations, and best practices to protect against cyber threats and unauthorized access.

Key components of system hardening may include:

- **Operating System Configuration**: Securely configuring operating system settings, services, and features to eliminate unnecessary functionalities and minimize exposure to potential security risks.
- **Patch Management**: Regularly applying security patches, updates, and fixes to address known vulnerabilities and software flaws that could be exploited by attackers.
- **Access Controls**: Implementing strong authentication mechanisms, access controls, and privilege management to restrict access to sensitive resources and ensure that only authorized users have appropriate permissions.
- **Network Security**: Deploying firewalls, intrusion detection and prevention systems (IDS/IPS), and other network security controls to monitor and control network traffic, detect suspicious activities, and prevent unauthorized access.
- **Encryption**: Enabling encryption for data in transit and at rest to protect sensitive information from eavesdropping, interception, or unauthorized access.
- **Auditing and Logging**: Implementing robust logging and auditing mechanisms to track and monitor system activities, detect security incidents, and facilitate forensic analysis and incident response.
- **Security Policies and Procedures**: Establishing comprehensive security policies, guidelines, and procedures to govern system configuration, user behavior, incident response, and security best practices.

Overall, system hardening is a proactive approach to strengthening the security posture of computer systems and networks, enhancing resilience against cyber threats, and safeguarding sensitive data and critical assets from exploitation and compromise.

**What are the several indicators of compromise that organizations should monitor?**

Indicators of Compromise (IOCs) are signs or evidence that a security incident may have occurred or that an organization's systems or networks may have been compromised by malicious activity. Monitoring IOCs is essential for detecting and responding to cybersecurity incidents effectively. Several common indicators of compromise that organizations should monitor include:

- **Anomalies in Network Traffic**: Unusual patterns or spikes in network traffic, such as unexpected data transfers, connections to suspicious IP addresses, or unusual protocols or ports being used, may indicate unauthorized access or data exfiltration.
- **Unusual System Behavior**: Signs of abnormal behavior on systems or endpoints, such as unexpected changes in file permissions, modifications to critical system files, or unauthorized access attempts, could indicate the presence of malware or unauthorized activity.
- **Security Alerts and Warnings**: Alerts generated by security tools, intrusion detection systems (IDS), antivirus software, or security information and event management (SIEM) systems indicating potential security incidents, such as malware detections, system compromises, or suspicious activities.
- **Phishing Attempts and Social Engineering**: Indications of phishing emails, spear-phishing attacks, or social engineering attempts targeting employees or users, such as suspicious email attachments, phishing URLs, or requests for sensitive information, may signal attempts to gain unauthorized access to systems or data.
- **System and Application Logs**: Analysis of system logs, event logs, and application logs for unusual or suspicious activities, such as failed login attempts, privilege escalations, or unauthorized access, can help detect security incidents and identify potential threats.
- **Excessive Account Privileges**: Instances of user accounts with excessive or unnecessary privileges, unauthorized access to privileged accounts, or unusual user behavior, such as logging in from unfamiliar locations or outside of normal business hours, may indicate insider threats or compromised accounts.
- **Unexplained Data Loss or Theft**: Evidence of unauthorized data access, data exfiltration, or data loss, such as missing or

corrupted files, unauthorized changes to data, or unexpected data transfers, could indicate a security breach or data breach incident.

**What are the status codes that a Web Application can return?**

1xx – Informational responses

2xx – Success

3xx – Redirection

4xx – Client-side error

5xx – Server-side error

**Describe traceroute and its purpose.**

Traceroute is a utility revealing the path taken by a packet, highlighting each intermediate point (usually routers) traversed. It's utilized primarily when packet delivery fails to reach its intended destination. Traceroute helps pinpoint where connectivity issues arise, aiding in identifying failure points.

**Distinguish between HIDS and NIDS.**

Host IDS (HIDS) and Network IDS (NIDS) both serve the purpose of detecting intrusions. The key disparity lies in their deployment: HIDS operates on specific hosts/devices, monitoring their traffic and system activities, while NIDS is network-centric, scrutinizing traffic across all devices within a network.

**What measures would you implement to secure a server?**

Securing servers involves utilizing SSL protocol for data encryption and decryption to prevent unauthorized data interception. Here are four fundamental steps:

1. Ensure Secure Passwords: Set strong passwords for root and administrator users.

2. Create New Users: Establish additional users for system management.

3. Disable Remote Access: Remove remote access from default root/administrator accounts.

4. Configure Firewall Rules: Set up firewall rules to regulate remote access.

## Define Data Leakage.

Data Leakage refers to the inadvertent or deliberate transmission of data from within an organization to an unauthorized external destination, compromising confidential information. It can occur accidentally, intentionally, or through system hacking techniques. Preventive measures, such as DLP (Data Leakage Prevention) Tools, can mitigate Data Leakage risks.

## Enumerate common Cyberattacks.

Several common cyberattacks pose significant threats to systems:

- Malware
- Phishing
- Password Attacks
- DDoS (Distributed Denial of Service)
- Man-in-the-Middle Attacks
- Drive-By Downloads
- Malvertising
- Rogue Software

## Types of Port Scanning?

Port Scanning is a method employed to detect open ports and services accessible on a host. Cybercriminals utilize port scanning to gather data useful for exploiting vulnerabilities, while administrators employ it to validate network security policies. Various Port Scanning Techniques include:

- Ping Scan

- TCP Half-Open
- TCP Connect
- UDP
- Stealth Scanning

How can identity theft be avoided?

To prevent identity theft, consider the following measures:

- Employ robust and distinctive passwords
- Refrain from disclosing sensitive details online, particularly on social networking platforms
- Patronize reputable and familiar online merchants
- Utilize up-to-date versions of web browsers
- Deploy advanced malware and spyware detection tools
- Implement specialized security software for financial information
- Regularly update both your system and software
- Safeguard your Social Security Number (SSN)


## Explain DDOS attack and how to prevent it

A DDOS (Distributed Denial of Service) attack disrupts server operations, preventing genuine clients from accessing services. These attacks fall into two main categories:

1. Flooding attacks: Hackers overwhelm the server with a massive volume of traffic, causing it to become unresponsive. Automated programs are often used to continuously send packets to the server.
2. Crash attacks: Hackers exploit vulnerabilities in the server's system, causing it to crash and rendering services inaccessible to clients.

To mitigate DDOS attacks, several preventive measures can be implemented:

- Utilize Anti-DDOS services designed to detect and mitigate such attacks.

- Configure Firewalls and Routers to filter and block malicious traffic.
- Deploy Front-End Hardware, such as intrusion prevention systems (IPS), to intercept and block attack traffic before reaching the server.
- Implement Load Balancing to evenly distribute incoming traffic across multiple servers, reducing the impact of DDOS attacks.
- Prepare to Handle Spikes in Traffic by scaling up server resources or leveraging cloud-based solutions to accommodate sudden increases in demand.
- What is ARP and how does it function?
- Address Resolution Protocol (ARP) is a networking protocol used to associate an IP address with a physical machine address within a local network.
- When a gateway receives an incoming packet intended for a host machine on the local area network, it triggers the ARP protocol to find the corresponding physical or MAC address associated with the IP address.
- The ARP program searches the ARP cache, and if a match is found, it provides the physical address to format the packet correctly and forward it to the intended machine.
- In cases where there is no entry for the IP address in the cache, ARP broadcasts a request packet to all machines on the LAN in a specialized format, seeking a response from any machine that may be associated with the IP address.

## What is 2FA and how can it be implemented for public websites?

What is two-factor authentication (2FA), and how can it be integrated into public websites?

Two-factor authentication (2FA) is a security process that requires users to provide two different authentication factors to verify their identity. These factors typically fall into three categories:

1. **Knowledge factors:** Something the user knows, such as a password or PIN.
2. **Possession factors:** Something the user has, such as a mobile device or security token.

3. **Inherence factors:** Something the user is, such as biometric data like fingerprints or facial recognition.

Implementing 2FA for public websites involves adding an extra layer of security beyond the traditional username and password combination. Here's how it can be implemented:

1. **Text Message (SMS) Verification:** After entering their username and password, users receive a one-time code via SMS to their registered mobile phone number. They then enter this code on the website to complete the login process.
2. **Email Verification:** Similar to SMS verification, users receive a one-time code via email after entering their credentials. They must then enter this code on the website to gain access.
3. **Authentication Apps:** Users can install authentication apps like Google Authenticator or Authy on their mobile devices. After entering their username and password, they use the app to generate a one-time code, which they enter on the website.
4. **Hardware Tokens:** Some websites may provide users with physical hardware tokens that generate one-time codes. Users enter these codes along with their credentials to authenticate.
5. **Biometric Verification:** For enhanced security, websites can incorporate biometric authentication methods such as fingerprint or facial recognition through compatible devices.

To implement 2FA on public websites, developers typically integrate authentication APIs or SDKs provided by authentication service providers. These services handle the generation and verification of one-time codes, making the implementation process more straightforward for website owners. Additionally, website administrators must ensure clear communication with users regarding the 2FA setup process and provide support for users who may encounter difficulties.

ENTRY LEVEL TECHNICAL QUESTIONS

## Define cybersecurity and its significance.

Cybersecurity is the practice of protecting computer systems, networks, and data from unauthorized access, damage, or theft. It plays a crucial role in safeguarding sensitive information, preserving privacy, preventing financial losses, and securing critical infrastructure against cyber threats.

**Define Virus, Malware, and Ransomware.**

- Virus: A program that replicates itself and spreads to other files or systems, often causing harm to computer systems.
- Malware: A broad term referring to any malicious software designed to disrupt, damage, or gain unauthorized access to computer systems or networks.
- Ransomware: A type of malware that encrypts files or computer systems and demands payment (ransom) for their decryption.

3. Explain the distinctions between Threat, Vulnerability, and Risk in cybersecurity.

- Threat: Any potential danger or harmful event that can exploit vulnerabilities and compromise security.
- Vulnerability: Weaknesses or gaps in security measures that could be exploited by threats to compromise systems or data.
- Risk: The likelihood of a threat exploiting a vulnerability and the potential impact or harm it may cause to an organization's security.

**Define Phishing and provide an example.**

Phishing is a cyberattack technique in which attackers use deceptive emails or messages to trick individuals into revealing sensitive information or performing actions that compromise security. For example, an attacker may send an email impersonating a legitimate bank, asking recipients to provide their login credentials by clicking on a fraudulent link that leads to a fake website.

**How do firewalls protect network security?**

Firewalls act as protective barriers that monitor and filter both incoming and outgoing network traffic based on predetermined security rules. They help prevent unauthorized access to a network, block malicious data packets, and mitigate potential cyber threats by enforcing security policies.

## What is a VPN, and why is it utilized?

A Virtual Private Network (VPN) is a technology that establishes a secure, encrypted connection over a public network, such as the internet. VPNs are used to enhance privacy, anonymity, and security by encrypting data traffic, protecting it from interception or eavesdropping. They allow users to access restricted content, secure public Wi-Fi connections, and maintain confidentiality while browsing online.

## Define a secure Password.

A secure password is a complex and unique combination of characters, including uppercase and lowercase letters, numbers, and special symbols. It should be lengthy and difficult to guess, reducing the likelihood of unauthorized access. Additionally, individuals should use different passwords for each account to minimize the risk of credential compromise in the event of a security breach.

## What are common techniques for securing a computer network?

Securing a computer network involves various techniques, including:

- Implementing strong password policies and user authentication mechanisms.
- Regularly updating and patching software and operating systems to address known vulnerabilities.
- Deploying firewalls, intrusion detection systems (IDS), and intrusion prevention systems (IPS) to monitor and protect network traffic.
- Conducting security audits and assessments to identify vulnerabilities and weaknesses.
- Encrypting sensitive data and communications to prevent unauthorized access or interception.
- Training employees on cybersecurity best practices and raising awareness of potential threats and risks.

## What is two-factor authentication, and why is it essential?

Two-factor authentication (2FA) is a security mechanism that requires users to provide two different forms of identification or verification to access an account or system. It enhances security by adding an additional layer of protection beyond passwords, reducing the risk of unauthorized access, credential theft, or identity fraud. Even if a password is compromised, 2FA prevents unauthorized access without the second factor, such as a unique code sent to a registered mobile device.

## Define Encryption and Decryption.

- Encryption: The process of converting plaintext data into ciphertext using cryptographic algorithms and keys to protect it from unauthorized access or interception.
- Decryption: The reverse process of encryption, which involves converting ciphertext back into its original plaintext form using the appropriate decryption key or algorithm.

## What is SSL encryption?

SSL (Secure Sockets Layer) encryption is a protocol used to secure and encrypt data transmitted between a web browser and a website server over the internet. It ensures the confidentiality and integrity of data by encrypting it during transmission, preventing unauthorized interception or tampering. SSL encryption is commonly employed in websites handling sensitive information, such as e-commerce platforms, banking websites, and online portals, to protect user data from unauthorized access or interception.

## How does IDS differ from IPS?

- IDS (Intrusion Detection System): IDS monitors network traffic and detects suspicious or malicious activity by analyzing traffic patterns, signatures, or anomalies. It generates alerts or notifications to alert security personnel of potential security incidents, but it does not take direct action to block or prevent attacks.
- IPS (Intrusion Prevention System): IPS performs the same functions as IDS but goes a step further by actively blocking or

preventing detected threats or attacks. It can automatically respond to security incidents by blocking malicious traffic, dropping suspicious packets, or reconfiguring firewall rules to mitigate potential threats.

## What is a security audit?

A security audit is a systematic evaluation or assessment of an organization's information systems, security policies, procedures, and controls to identify weaknesses, vulnerabilities, or compliance gaps. It examines the effectiveness of existing security measures, assesses the organization's security posture, and provides recommendations for improving security, enhancing resilience, and mitigating risks. Security audits help organizations identify security threats, protect sensitive data, and ensure regulatory compliance with industry standards and regulations.

## What steps should be taken in response to a security breach?

In response to a security breach, organizations should take the following steps:

- Immediately isolate and contain the affected systems or networks to prevent further damage or spread of the breach.
- Notify relevant stakeholders, including internal security teams, management, legal counsel, and regulatory authorities, as required by applicable laws or regulations.
- Initiate a thorough investigation to determine the scope, impact, and root cause of the breach, preserving evidence and documenting findings for forensic analysis.
- Remediate vulnerabilities or security gaps identified during the investigation, such as patching software, updating configurations, or enhancing security controls.

INTERMEDIATE LEVEL TECHNICAL QUESTIONS

## Elucidate the concept of Public Key Infrastructure (PKI).

Public Key Infrastructure (PKI) constitutes a cryptographic framework facilitating secure communication across untrusted networks. It relies on a pair of cryptographic keys – a public key and a private key – for various operations like encryption, decryption, digital signatures, and the validation of public keys. Certificate Authorities (CAs) are integral to PKI, ensuring the legitimacy of public keys through the issuance of digital certificates.

## What are the essential components of a robust security policy?

A robust security policy encompasses key elements such as access controls, encryption protocols, regular system updates, comprehensive user training, well-defined incident response plans, and adherence to relevant regulatory requirements.

## Describe the functionality of a rootkit and methods for its detection.

A rootkit is malicious software designed to grant unauthorized access to a computer or network, often operating stealthily to evade detection. Detection techniques typically involve utilizing specialized anti-rootkit tools, monitoring for anomalous system behavior, and conducting thorough system scans to identify and remove rootkit infections.

## Define cross-site scripting (XSS) and SQL injection vulnerabilities.

Cross-site scripting (XSS) involves injecting malicious scripts into web applications, enabling attackers to execute unauthorized actions or steal sensitive information from users. SQL injection exploits vulnerabilities in SQL queries to manipulate databases, potentially leading to data breaches or system compromises. Both XSS and SQL injection are common forms of web application vulnerabilities.

## What characterizes a zero-day vulnerability?

A zero-day vulnerability refers to a security flaw in software or hardware that is unknown to the vendor and lacks an available patch or solution. This vulnerability poses a significant risk as it can be exploited by attackers before developers develop a fix, leaving systems vulnerable to exploitation.

## Discuss the ISO 27001/27002 standards.

ISO 27001 establishes the requirements for an Information Security Management System (ISMS), providing a framework for organizations to manage and mitigate security risks effectively. ISO 27002 offers guidelines for implementing security controls and best practices within an organization, helping to ensure the confidentiality, integrity, and availability of information assets.

## How do threat detection systems operate?

Threat detection systems analyze network traffic and system logs in real-time to identify suspicious activities or potential security threats. They employ predefined rules, behavioral analytics, and machine learning algorithms to detect anomalies indicative of malicious behavior, enabling organizations to respond swiftly to security incidents.

## Explain the principles underlying ethical hacking.

Ethical hacking involves legally testing systems and networks for vulnerabilities to strengthen security defenses. Key principles include obtaining proper authorization before conducting assessments, maintaining confidentiality of sensitive information, adhering to ethical guidelines and legal frameworks, and responsibly disclosing any identified vulnerabilities to relevant stakeholders.

## Enumerate the various types of network security measures.

Network security encompasses a range of measures, including perimeter security mechanisms, such as firewalls and intrusion detection/prevention systems (IDS/IPS), virtual private networks (VPNs) for secure remote access, encryption protocols to protect data in transit, and network segmentation to isolate and contain potential threats. These measures collectively safeguard network infrastructure, data, and resources against unauthorized access and malicious activities.

**Elaborate on the concept of risk assessment in cybersecurity.**

In the realm of cybersecurity, risk assessment entails the systematic process of recognizing, evaluating, and prioritizing potential threats and vulnerabilities to make informed decisions regarding the implementation of appropriate security measures.

**Define incident response and its management approach.**

Incident response refers to the structured approach employed for managing and mitigating security incidents within an organization. This multifaceted process encompasses various stages, including preparation, detection, containment, eradication, recovery, and post-incident analysis.

**Explain the principle of least privilege.**

The principle of least privilege advocates for restricting users' and processes' access rights to the minimum level necessary to fulfill their specific tasks or functions. By limiting privileges, organizations reduce the likelihood of unauthorized access and mitigate the impact of potential security breaches.

**How does Secure Socket Layer (SSL) function?**

SSL operates by facilitating secure communication between web browsers and servers through the implementation of encryption, authentication, and data integrity mechanisms. It ensures the confidentiality and integrity of transmitted data, thereby safeguarding sensitive information from unauthorized interception or tampering.

**Define network sniffing and its implications.**

Network sniffing involves intercepting and analyzing network traffic to extract information, often for monitoring purposes or malicious activities. It poses significant security risks as it can expose sensitive data, including login credentials, financial information, or proprietary business data, to unauthorized entities.

**Discuss the significance of disaster recovery planning in cybersecurity.**

Disaster recovery planning is crucial in cybersecurity as it entails proactive measures and contingency strategies aimed at mitigating the impact of potential data breaches, system failures, or catastrophic events. By establishing robust recovery protocols, organizations can minimize downtime, prevent data loss, and ensure business continuity in the face of unforeseen disasters.

## What is a Security Information and Event Management (SIEM) System?

A Security Information and Event Management (SIEM) system is a comprehensive security solution that aggregates, correlates, and analyzes data from various sources to detect and respond to security incidents effectively. It provides organizations with real-time insights into their security posture and enables proactive threat detection and response capabilities.

## How do you handle cryptographic keys securely?

Managing cryptographic keys involves securely generating, storing, distributing, and revoking encryption keys to safeguard sensitive data and maintain the confidentiality and integrity of encrypted communications. Employing robust key management practices is essential to prevent unauthorized access or misuse of cryptographic keys.

## Enumerate common methods for secure data disposal.

Secure data disposal methods include data shredding, overwriting, degaussing, and physical destruction of storage media. These techniques ensure that sensitive information is irreversibly erased from storage devices, thereby mitigating the risk of data breaches or unauthorized data retrieval.

## Define endpoint security and its significance.

Endpoint security pertains to the protection of individual computing devices such as computers and mobile devices from cyber threats. It encompasses the deployment of antivirus, anti-malware, and intrusion detection systems to safeguard endpoints against malicious activities and unauthorized access.

**Explore the role of artificial intelligence (AI) in cybersecurity.**

AI plays a pivotal role in cybersecurity by enabling advanced threat detection, pattern recognition, and anomaly detection capabilities. It enhances cybersecurity defenses by automating incident response processes, augmenting human decision-making, and identifying emerging threats in real-time.

**Enumerate the challenges associated with cloud security.**

Cloud security challenges encompass a wide range of concerns, including data breaches, compliance requirements, data loss prevention, and the complexity of securing shared responsibility models in cloud environments. Addressing these challenges requires robust security measures and adherence to best practices for cloud security management.

**Differentiate between penetration testing and vulnerability assessments.**

Penetration testing involves simulating real-world cyber attacks to identify vulnerabilities and assess the effectiveness of security controls. In contrast, vulnerability assessments focus on scanning systems and networks to detect known vulnerabilities and weaknesses. Both techniques are essential for identifying and mitigating security risks proactively.

**Define the function of a Security Operations Center (SOC).**

A Security Operations Center (SOC) serves as a centralized hub responsible for real-time monitoring, detection, and response to cybersecurity incidents. It operates round-the-clock to identify and mitigate security threats, coordinate incident response efforts, and enhance overall cybersecurity posture.

**Highlight the significance of compliance in cybersecurity.**

Compliance ensures that organizations adhere to relevant laws, regulations, and industry standards governing data security and privacy. Compliance measures help protect sensitive data, mitigate risks, and avoid legal consequences associated with non-compliance.

Additionally, compliance frameworks provide guidelines for implementing robust cybersecurity practices and maintaining data integrity.

## Explain multi-factor authentication (MFA) and its security benefits.

Multi-factor authentication (MFA) enhances security by requiring users to provide multiple authentication factors during the login process. These factors typically include something the user knows (e.g., a password) and something they possess (e.g., a mobile token). MFA helps mitigate the risk of unauthorized access by adding an extra layer of security beyond traditional password-based authentication methods.

### ADVANCED TECHNICAL QUESTIONS

## Explore the difficulties and approaches to securing IoT devices.

Challenges: Variability in devices, resource limitations, and susceptibility to vulnerabilities. Strategies: Implement regular updates, enforce robust authentication mechanisms, utilize network segmentation, and adhere to established IoT security frameworks.

## Define Advanced Persistent Threats (APTs).

APTs denote prolonged, targeted cyber assaults orchestrated by adept adversaries. They leverage stealth, persistence, and sophisticated methodologies to infiltrate systems clandestinely.

## Examine the role of blockchain in cybersecurity.

Blockchain technology enhances security by facilitating decentralized consensus mechanisms, ensuring data integrity, and maintaining immutable transaction records. It finds applications in secure transactions and identity verification.

**How do you handle security for a sprawling, decentralized network?**

Adopt segmentation strategies, enforce stringent access controls, conduct routine audits, and deploy continuous network monitoring to fortify defenses against threats across an expansive network infrastructure.

**Highlight the significance of forensic analysis in cybersecurity.**

Forensic analysis plays a pivotal role in investigating security incidents, collecting evidence, and comprehending attack vectors. It facilitates incident response efforts and aids in legal proceedings by providing insights into malicious activities.

**Delve into the complexities of network protocol security.**

Ensuring the security of network protocols is paramount for preserving data confidentiality and integrity. Employ encryption mechanisms, implement robust authentication protocols, and prioritize regular protocol updates to mitigate potential security risks.

**How do you integrate security measures within a DevOps framework?**

Integrate security practices seamlessly into the DevOps pipeline through automation, continuous monitoring, and fostering collaboration between development and security teams. This approach ensures that security is prioritized throughout the software development lifecycle.

**Elaborate on the concept of micro-segmentation in network security.**

Micro-segmentation involves partitioning network segments into smaller, isolated zones to enhance control and security measures. By restricting the lateral movement of threats within a network, micro-segmentation helps minimize the potential impact of security breaches.

**Explore the obstacles associated with safeguarding big data environments.**

Challenges encompass the vast volume and heterogeneity of data. Mitigation strategies entail implementing robust encryption mechanisms, enforcing stringent access controls, employing proactive monitoring solutions, and implementing comprehensive data classification frameworks.

**Outline your approaches for mitigating supply chain risks in cybersecurity.**

Conduct thorough assessments of third-party vendors, enforce adherence to established security standards, execute regular audits to evaluate compliance, and establish a robust supply chain risk management framework to proactively address potential vulnerabilities and threats.

**Define the concept of container security.**

Enhance the security posture of containerized applications by implementing measures such as image scanning to detect vulnerabilities, enforcing granular access controls, and deploying runtime protection mechanisms to prevent exploitation of weaknesses.

**How do you ensure adherence to international data protection regulations like GDPR?**

Adopt proactive measures such as formulating and implementing comprehensive data protection policies, conducting thorough privacy impact assessments, and ensuring compliance with consent requirements and data subject rights stipulated by relevant regulations like GDPR.

**Analyze forthcoming trends in cybersecurity.**

Anticipated trends encompass the utilization of artificial intelligence and machine learning algorithms for enhanced threat detection capabilities, the adoption of zero-trust architecture to bolster network security, increased emphasis on cloud security measures, and heightened focus on addressing security challenges posed by the proliferation of IoT and 5G technologies.

## Examine the ethical considerations inherent in cybersecurity practices.

Ethical dilemmas revolve around safeguarding individual and organizational privacy, adhering to principles of responsible disclosure when identifying vulnerabilities, and minimizing potential harm to stakeholders.

## How do you assess the efficacy of a cybersecurity initiative?

Evaluate the effectiveness of a cybersecurity program by leveraging metrics such as the outcomes of risk assessments, response times during security incidents, and periodic evaluations of the organization's overall security posture.

## Discuss the complexities associated with fortifying wireless networks.

Challenges include the presence of rogue access points and the susceptibility to eavesdropping attacks. Address these concerns by implementing robust encryption protocols, deploying comprehensive network monitoring solutions, and educating users about best practices for wireless network security.

## Define quantum cryptography and its implications for security.

Quantum cryptography leverages principles of quantum mechanics to secure communication channels. It offers the potential to withstand attacks facilitated by quantum computers, ensuring the long-term integrity and confidentiality of sensitive information transmitted over quantum-resistant cryptographic protocols.

**Elucidate the notion of federated identity management.**

Federated identity management streamlines access to multiple systems using a unified set of credentials, simplifying user authentication while bolstering security measures.

**What are the recent advancements in cybersecurity threats?**

Emerging threats encompass novel attack vectors like supply chain infiltrations, ransomware schemes, and sophisticated AI-driven assaults.

**How do you ensure security in a hybrid cloud infrastructure?**

Ensure the robustness of hybrid cloud security through the consistent application of security protocols, meticulous identity management, and rigorous data protection measures spanning both on-premises and cloud-based resources.

**Delve into the influence of artificial intelligence on cybersecurity challenges.**

AI technologies have the potential to revolutionize cybersecurity by automating threat detection processes, refining incident response mechanisms, and enhancing the efficacy of security analytics. Nonetheless, there's also a looming risk of adversaries exploiting AI for malicious intents.

**What role does machine learning play in identifying cyber threats?**

Machine learning algorithms sift through extensive datasets to identify irregular patterns and anomalies indicative of potential cyber threats, empowering organizations to proactively mitigate security risks.

**Elaborate on the concept of threat intelligence and its practical utility.**

Threat intelligence involves gathering and analyzing data to detect and preempt emerging threats, furnishing organizations with actionable insights to fortify their cybersecurity posture and preclude potential security breaches.

## How would you fortify mobile applications against security vulnerabilities?

Bolster the security of mobile apps through the implementation of robust encryption mechanisms, meticulous code reviews, secure API integrations, and regular updates to promptly address identified vulnerabilities and forestall data breaches.

### Personal Cybersecurity Interview Questions

Possessing the necessary technical skills and qualifications is crucial, but having the appropriate personality to mesh well with a company's culture or a team's dynamics is equally important for a top-notch Cyber Security Analyst.

Below is a sample question on personal approach and a strategy for answering it during a cybersecurity interview:

## How do you stay informed about developments and trends in the cybersecurity field?

Keeping abreast of the latest trends and news in cybersecurity is pivotal for effectively safeguarding an organization against new vulnerabilities and threats. When discussing your approach with the hiring manager, emphasize your routine of monitoring vulnerability notification feeds and security advisories, reading articles from leading cybersecurity news outlets and blogs, and engaging with prominent cybersecurity figures on social media platforms. Additionally, highlight your involvement in the cybersecurity community, whether through attending conferences, participating in live events, or joining forums and discussions with peers in the field. This not only shows your dedication to continuous learning but also your commitment to contributing to and learning from the broader cybersecurity community.

**Which trend in cybersecurity are you most excited about?**
The trend that excites me most in cybersecurity is the increasing integration of artificial intelligence (AI) and machine learning (ML) technologies. AI and ML are revolutionizing how we detect and respond to threats by analyzing massive datasets more efficiently than humanly possible, predicting threats, and automating responses. This technology not only enhances threat detection capabilities but also significantly reduces response times to incidents, making cybersecurity measures more proactive and less reactive.

**Which cybersecurity trend will have the biggest impact in five years?**
In the next five years, I believe the zero-trust architecture will have the most significant impact on cybersecurity. As organizations continue to evolve with more remote work and cloud-based resources, traditional security perimeters are becoming obsolete. Zero-trust principles, which require verifying anything and everything trying to connect to a system before granting access, regardless of whether it is inside or outside the network, will fundamentally change how organizations approach security, making it more adaptive and resilient against breaches.

**What is an emerging threat in cybersecurity that deserves more attention?**
Supply chain attacks are an emerging threat that I believe deserves more attention. As organizations increasingly rely on third-party vendors and software, attackers are exploiting these relationships to bypass traditional security measures. These attacks can compromise multiple organizations through a single breach of a supplier, as seen in high-profile incidents like the SolarWinds attack. Strengthening supply chain security requires a collaborative effort among all parties involved and an understanding that an organization's security is only as strong as the weakest link in its supply chain.

**Tell us about your preferred work environment.**

My preferred work environment is one that fosters collaboration, innovation, and continuous learning. I thrive in settings where team members are encouraged to share knowledge, challenge ideas, and work together to solve complex problems. A culture that values security as a collective responsibility and supports professional growth through opportunities to work on diverse projects, attend workshops, and gain new certifications is important to me. I also appreciate environments that offer flexibility in work arrangements, recognizing the importance of work-life balance.

**Tell us about your educational background. How has your education prepared you for this job?**

I hold a degree in Information Security, which provided me with a solid foundation in the principles of cybersecurity, including network security, cryptography, and ethical hacking. My coursework included hands-on labs and projects that simulated real-world cybersecurity challenges, allowing me to apply theoretical knowledge to practical situations. Additionally, I have pursued various cybersecurity certifications to specialize further and stay current in this rapidly evolving field. This blend of academic knowledge and practical experience has equipped me with the critical thinking and technical skills necessary to identify and mitigate cyber threats effectively.

**What extracurricular activities do you participate in?**

Outside of my professional interests, I engage in several extracurricular activities that contribute to my personal and professional growth. I am an active member of a local cybersecurity meetup group where we share knowledge, discuss the latest trends, and occasionally organize workshops or capture-the-flag competitions. I also volunteer my time to mentor students interested in pursuing careers in cybersecurity, helping them navigate their educational and professional paths. Additionally, I enjoy participating in outdoor activities, such as hiking and cycling, which help me maintain a healthy work-life balance and provide a fresh perspective on problem-solving.

## 1. Incident Response Scenario

**Question**: "Imagine you are part of our cybersecurity team, and you've just been alerted to a potential breach where sensitive customer data may have been accessed. Walk us through the steps you would take from the moment you're notified of the breach to the resolution of the incident."

When responding to this question in a cybersecurity job interview, a strong answer would showcase your systematic approach to incident response, emphasizing quick action, thorough investigation, communication, and a focus on long-term solutions to prevent future incidents. Here's a structured response that covers these key points:

### Initial Response and Assessment:

1. **Immediate Containment**: My first action would be to isolate the affected systems to prevent further data exfiltration or damage. This may involve temporarily disconnecting them from the network, depending on the nature of the breach.
2. **Preliminary Assessment**: Quickly gather initial details about the breach, including which systems are affected, the type of data accessed, and any potential entry points for the attackers. This helps in understanding the scope and urgency of the situation.

### In-depth Investigation:

3. **Forensic Analysis**: Using forensic tools and techniques, I would perform a deep dive to trace the attackers' movements, identify how they gained access, and ascertain the full extent of the data compromised. This step is crucial for understanding the breach's specifics and preventing similar incidents.
4. **Eradication and Recovery**: Once we've identified the breach's source, the next step would be to remove the attackers' access to our systems. This could involve patching vulnerabilities, changing passwords, and implementing more

stringent access controls. Following eradication, we would restore the affected systems from backups, ensuring no compromised data is reintroduced.

**Post-Incident Actions:**

5. **Notification and Communication**: Communicate with all relevant stakeholders, including management, affected customers, and potentially law enforcement, in accordance with legal and regulatory requirements. Transparency is key, so I'd ensure the communication is clear about what happened, the potential impact, and the steps being taken to resolve the issue and protect against future breaches.
6. **Review and Improve Security Posture**: Conduct a thorough review of the incident to identify lessons learned and any gaps in the existing security measures. This would involve reviewing and updating the incident response plan to incorporate new insights and strategies to prevent recurrence.
7. **Ongoing Monitoring and Prevention**: Increase monitoring of network traffic and system logs to detect any signs of lingering issues or another breach attempt. Implement additional security measures as necessary, such as more sophisticated intrusion detection systems, enhanced encryption, and employee training on security awareness.

This answer demonstrates a comprehensive and methodical approach to handling a data breach, emphasizing the importance of quick containment, thorough investigation, clear communication, and ongoing improvements to security practices. Tailoring the response to reflect specific skills or experiences can further strengthen your answer.

### 2. Phishing Attack Scenario

**Question**: "Suppose an employee in the finance department receives an email that appears to be from the CEO, asking for an urgent wire transfer. The employee suspects it might be a phishing attempt. As a cybersecurity specialist, how would you handle the situation?

Describe the process you would follow to investigate and advise the employee."

When faced with a potential phishing attempt like the one described, a comprehensive response would highlight your ability to act swiftly to verify the legitimacy of the request, safeguard sensitive information, and educate employees to prevent future incidents. Here's how you might structure a detailed answer:

**Immediate Verification and Containment:**

1. **Direct Verification**: Advise the employee not to respond to the email or take any action requested in the message. Instead, suggest verifying the request's authenticity by contacting the CEO or the executive mentioned in the email directly, using a known and trusted communication method, such as a phone call, to confirm if the request is legitimate.
2. **Email Analysis**: Examine the suspicious email for common signs of phishing, including the sender's email address, language used, and any links or attachments in the email. Check if the email address domain matches the company's domain exactly or if there are subtle misspellings designed to deceive.

**In-depth Investigation and Reporting:**

3. **Incident Reporting**: Report the incident to the company's cybersecurity team for further analysis. This would include capturing all relevant information about the email, such as headers, which can provide insights into the email's origin and path.
4. **Forensic Analysis**: If equipped to do so, perform a forensic analysis of the email to identify any malicious payload or links. This could involve analyzing the email in a secure environment to understand the attacker's methods without risking the company's network.

**Preventive Actions and Education:**

5. **Strengthen Email Filters**: Based on the findings, update the email filtering rules to better catch similar phishing attempts

in the future. This might involve adding rules to flag emails with certain keywords, from similar spoofed domains, or with suspicious attachments.

6. **Employee Training and Awareness**: Organize a training session or send a communication to all employees highlighting this attempted phishing attack as a case study. Emphasize the importance of vigilance when handling email requests for sensitive actions, such as wire transfers, and encourage them to verify unusual requests through secondary communication channels.

7. **Review and Update Policies**: Review and possibly update the company's financial authorization procedures and cybersecurity policies to include stronger verification processes for requests involving sensitive actions. This might involve multi-factor authentication, a callback procedure, or requiring multiple approvals for significant financial transactions.

8. **Ongoing Monitoring and Response**: Monitor for further suspicious activity and remain vigilant for similar or more sophisticated phishing attempts. Ensure that there are clear procedures in place for employees to report suspicious emails and requests, facilitating a quick response to potential threats.

This answer showcases a proactive and multi-faceted approach to managing and mitigating phishing threats, emphasizing direct action, in-depth investigation, preventive measures, and the importance of employee education in maintaining cybersecurity.

### 3. Malware Infection Scenario

**Question**: "You've detected unusual network traffic indicating a possible malware infection on several workstations. How would you approach this situation to identify the infected systems, contain the malware, and prevent further infections? Please describe the tools and techniques you would use."

In responding to a scenario involving unusual network traffic and a potential malware infection, it's essential to demonstrate a systematic approach that covers identification, containment, eradication, and prevention. Here's how you could structure a comprehensive answer:

**Initial Identification and Containment:**

1. **Network Traffic Analysis**: First, I would use network monitoring tools, such as Wireshark or SolarWinds, to analyze the suspicious traffic patterns. By examining the source, destination, and type of traffic, I can pinpoint abnormal activities that may indicate malware communication to external servers.

2. **System Identification**: Utilize endpoint detection and response (EDR) tools, like CrowdStrike Falcon or Microsoft Defender for Endpoint, to identify the workstations exhibiting unusual behavior. These tools can help trace the source of the malware by analyzing system logs, running processes, and file changes.

3. **Isolation of Affected Systems**: To prevent the spread of the malware, I would isolate the affected workstations from the network. This could involve disconnecting them from the Wi-Fi or LAN and blocking their access at the network level through the firewall or network access control (NAC) system.

**In-depth Investigation and Eradication:**

4. **Forensic Analysis**: On the isolated systems, conduct a forensic analysis to understand how the malware operates, its persistence mechanisms, and the extent of the infection. Tools such as Malwarebytes, Kaspersky Virus Removal Tool, or custom scripts can be used for deep scanning and analysis.

5. **Identify the Entry Point**: Determine how the malware was introduced to the network. This could involve reviewing email logs, web access logs, or user reports to find the initial vector, whether it be a phishing email, compromised website, or malicious download.

6. **Eradication of Malware**: Utilize antivirus and anti-malware tools to remove the malware from the infected systems. In cases where automated tools are insufficient, manual removal might be necessary, based on the forensic analysis findings.

### Recovery and Prevention:

7. **System Restoration**: Restore the affected systems using known good backups after ensuring the malware is completely removed. Test the systems in an isolated environment before reconnecting them to the network.
8. **Update Security Measures**: Based on the findings from the investigation, update antivirus signatures, firewall rules, and intrusion detection/prevention systems (IDS/IPS) to detect and block the specific malware and similar threats in the future.
9. **User Education and Policy Update**: Conduct training sessions for users to recognize and avoid malicious activities, such as phishing attempts. Review and update security policies to strengthen the organization's defense against future infections. This might include stricter email filtering, enhanced endpoint protection, and regular security awareness training.
10. **Ongoing Monitoring**: Increase monitoring of network and system activity to quickly detect and respond to unusual behavior that may indicate a new infection. Utilize a Security Information and Event Management (SIEM) system, like Splunk or LogRhythm, for real-time analysis and alerts.

This response highlights a comprehensive approach to dealing with malware infections, emphasizing thorough investigation, effective containment and eradication, and the importance of preventive measures and ongoing vigilance. Tailoring the answer to include specific tools and techniques you're familiar with can further demonstrate your expertise and readiness to handle such situations.

### 4. Insider Threat Scenario

**Question**: "An internal audit has revealed that confidential files have been unexpectedly accessed and copied to an external device. As part of the cybersecurity team, describe the steps you would take to investigate this incident, identify the responsible party, and prevent such breaches in the future."

Addressing an incident where confidential files have been accessed and copied requires a methodical approach to investigate the breach, identify the perpetrator, and implement measures to prevent future incidents. Here's a structured response to tackle such a scenario:

**Immediate Response and Investigation:**

1. **Audit Log Review**: Begin by examining detailed access and audit logs to track the unauthorized access or file copying activities. This includes reviewing logs from data loss prevention (DLP) systems, file servers, and endpoint security tools to pinpoint when and from where the files were accessed.
2. **User and Device Identification**: Use the logs to identify the user accounts and devices involved in the incident. This involves correlating times, IP addresses, and device identifiers to trace back to the specific workstations or external devices used.
3. **Forensic Analysis**: Conduct a forensic analysis of the involved devices to uncover any traces left by the unauthorized access, such as temporary files, system registry changes, or malware that facilitated the breach. Tools like EnCase or FTK can be instrumental in this phase.

**Containment and Eradication:**

4. **Isolate Affected Systems**: Temporarily isolate the implicated workstations or user accounts to prevent further unauthorized access or data exfiltration while the investigation is ongoing.
5. **Remove Unauthorized Access**: If the investigation reveals that specific accounts have been compromised or external devices have been maliciously used, take steps to revoke access permissions and secure the accounts or endpoints involved.

**Root Cause Analysis and Recovery:**

6. **Determine How the Breach Occurred**: Analyze how the unauthorized access was possible—whether through compromised credentials, insider threat, or a security vulnerability—and address the root cause to prevent recurrence.

7. **Restore Security Posture**: Ensure that any changes made by the unauthorized access are reverted and that all security measures are reinstated or enhanced as necessary. This might include changing affected passwords, patching vulnerabilities, and improving encryption of sensitive files.

**Preventive Measures and Policy Updates:**

8. **Enhance Monitoring and Alerting**: Implement or improve monitoring tools and set up alerts for unusual access patterns or large data transfers to quickly detect potential breaches in the future.

9. **User Access Review**: Conduct regular reviews of user access rights to ensure that employees only have the necessary permissions for their roles, minimizing the risk of both insider threats and the impact of compromised accounts.

10. **Employee Training and Awareness**: Enhance security awareness training for all employees to highlight the importance of protecting confidential information and recognizing potential security threats.

11. **Policy and Procedure Updates**: Update security policies and incident response procedures based on lessons learned from the incident. This may include stricter controls on the use of external storage devices, enhanced authentication protocols, and more rigorous audit trails.

**Review and Compliance:**

12. **Documentation and Reporting**: Document the incident thoroughly, including the investigation findings, actions taken, and preventive measures implemented. Report the breach to relevant stakeholders and comply with any legal or regulatory reporting obligations.

13. **Continuous Improvement**: Treat the incident as a learning opportunity. Regularly review and update security policies

and practices to adapt to evolving threats and ensure the organization's resilience against future incidents.

This structured response outlines a comprehensive approach to managing a data breach, emphasizing thorough investigation, immediate containment, and long-term preventive strategies. Tailoring this response to reflect specific tools or methodologies you're familiar with can further demonstrate your expertise.

### 5. Compliance and Security Framework Scenario

**Question**: "Your company is looking to achieve compliance with the General Data Protection Regulation (GDPR) due to its operations in Europe. As a cybersecurity expert, what measures would you recommend implementing to ensure compliance with GDPR's data protection requirements?"

Achieving compliance with the General Data Protection Regulation (GDPR) requires a comprehensive approach that encompasses various aspects of data protection, privacy policies, and cybersecurity practices. Here's a structured plan outlining the key measures and strategies to ensure GDPR compliance:

**Data Protection and Privacy Measures:**

1. **Data Inventory and Mapping**: Conduct a thorough inventory of all personal data your company holds, processes, or transfers. This includes identifying the type of data, its source, how it is processed, where it is stored, and to whom it is disclosed.
2. **Privacy Impact Assessments (PIAs)**: Perform regular Privacy Impact Assessments for processes that handle personal data to evaluate and mitigate risks to data subjects' privacy.
3. **Data Minimization and Purpose Limitation**: Ensure that only the minimum necessary personal data is collected for explicitly specified, legitimate purposes. Data should not be retained longer than necessary for its intended purposes.

## Technical and Organizational Measures:

4. **Encryption and Anonymization**: Implement encryption and anonymization techniques to protect data at rest and in transit. This reduces the risk of data breaches and the impact should a breach occur.
5. **Access Control and Authentication**: Enforce strict access control measures to ensure that only authorized personnel can access personal data. This includes using strong authentication mechanisms and maintaining detailed access logs.
6. **Data Breach Response Plan**: Develop and maintain a robust data breach response plan that outlines the procedures for detecting, reporting, and investigating a data breach. GDPR requires breaches to be reported to the relevant authority within 72 hours of discovery.

## Legal and Compliance Frameworks:

7. **Data Processing Agreements (DPAs)**: Review and update contracts with third parties (processors) that handle personal data on your behalf. Ensure these contracts include GDPR-compliant data processing agreements that define roles, responsibilities, and data protection standards.
8. **Data Protection Officer (DPO)**: Appoint a Data Protection Officer if your company's core activities require regular and systematic monitoring of data subjects on a large scale, or involve processing sensitive personal data. The DPO will oversee compliance with GDPR and act as a point of contact for data protection authorities.

## Training and Awareness:

9. **Employee Training**: Conduct regular training sessions for employees to raise awareness about GDPR requirements, data protection best practices, and the importance of privacy and security.

## Policies and Documentation:

10. **Privacy Policy and Notice Updates**: Update your privacy notices and policies to ensure transparency about how personal data is collected, used, and protected. Include information on data subjects' rights under GDPR and how they can exercise those rights.
11. **Consent Management**: Implement mechanisms to obtain and manage consent for data processing activities when consent is the legal basis for processing. Ensure that consent is freely given, specific, informed, and unambiguous.

## Monitoring and Continuous Improvement:

12. **Regular Audits and Compliance Checks**: Conduct regular audits to ensure ongoing compliance with GDPR. This includes reviewing and updating data protection measures, policies, and procedures as necessary.
13. **Engage with Regulators**: Maintain open communication with data protection authorities to ensure you are up-to-date with guidance, regulations, and best practices related to GDPR.

## 6. Cloud Security Scenario

**Question**: "The company is migrating its data to a cloud service provider. What are the key security considerations you would take into account to protect the data during and after the migration? How would you work with the cloud provider to ensure the security of the data?"

When migrating data to a cloud service provider, ensuring the security of the data both during the migration process and afterwards is crucial. This involves a combination of technical measures, due diligence, and ongoing collaboration with the cloud provider. Here's a structured approach to addressing these considerations:

## Pre-Migration Planning:

1. **Data Classification and Risk Assessment**: Before migration, classify the data to identify sensitive or regulated information and assess the risks associated with moving it to the cloud. This will help in determining the appropriate security controls.

2. **Choose the Right Cloud Service Model**: Decide between Infrastructure as a Service (IaaS), Platform as a Service (PaaS), or Software as a Service (SaaS) based on the level of control needed over the environment and the type of data being migrated.

3. **Cloud Provider Due Diligence**: Evaluate potential cloud providers for their security standards, compliance certifications (e.g., ISO 27001, SOC 2), and data protection policies. Ensure they align with your security requirements and regulatory obligations.

## During Migration:

4. **Secure Data Transfer**: Use encrypted communication channels (e.g., SSL/TLS) for transferring data to the cloud. Consider encrypting the data before the transfer, especially if it's sensitive.

5. **Access Controls**: Implement strict access controls and authentication mechanisms during the migration process to limit who can access the data. Use the principle of least privilege to minimize exposure.

6. **Data Integrity Checks**: Perform data integrity checks before, during, and after migration to ensure that the data has not been altered or corrupted. This might involve checksums or hashes to verify data integrity.

## Post-Migration Security Measures:

7. **Encryption**: Ensure that data is encrypted at rest and in transit within the cloud environment. Discuss with the cloud provider the encryption methods used and the management of encryption keys.

8. **Identity and Access Management (IAM)**: Work with the cloud provider to set up IAM policies that control user access

to cloud resources. Use multi-factor authentication (MFA) and role-based access controls (RBAC) to enhance security.

9. **Monitoring and Logging**: Set up continuous monitoring and logging of access to and activity around your cloud-stored data. This helps in detecting unauthorized access or data breaches.

## Ongoing Collaboration and Compliance:

10. **Regular Security Assessments**: Conduct regular security assessments and audits of your cloud environment to identify vulnerabilities and ensure compliance with relevant regulations and standards.

11. **Incident Response Plan**: Develop and maintain an incident response plan that includes procedures for responding to security incidents in the cloud. Coordinate with the cloud provider on their role in incident response.

12. **Data Backup and Recovery**: Implement a robust data backup and recovery strategy to protect against data loss. Ensure that backups are encrypted and stored securely.

13. **Legal and Regulatory Compliance**: Work closely with the cloud provider to ensure that data storage and processing practices comply with applicable laws and regulations, such as GDPR, HIPAA, or CCPA.

14. **SLAs and Contracts**: Ensure that service level agreements (SLAs) and contracts with the cloud provider clearly define the security responsibilities of each party and include provisions for protecting your data.

## 7. Zero-Day Vulnerability Scenario

**Question**: "A zero-day vulnerability has been announced in a widely used software application within your organization. Describe the steps you would take to mitigate the risk until a patch is available. How would you communicate this issue to the rest of the organization?"

Addressing a zero-day vulnerability in a widely used software application requires swift action to mitigate risks and clear communication to ensure organization-wide awareness and compliance with protective measures. Here's a step-by-step plan to manage the situation effectively:

**Immediate Response and Risk Assessment:**

1. **Initial Risk Assessment**: Quickly gather details about the vulnerability, including the affected software versions and the potential impact on your organization. Assess the risk based on the vulnerability's severity, exploitability, and the criticality of the affected systems.

2. **Temporary Workarounds and Mitigations**: Investigate and implement temporary workarounds or mitigations to reduce the risk. This could involve disabling certain features of the software, implementing network-level controls to block exploit traffic, or applying compensatory security controls.

3. **Isolate or Limit Access to Vulnerable Systems**: If practical, isolate vulnerable systems from the network or limit access to them until the vulnerability can be patched. This may help in reducing the potential attack surface.

**Patch Management and Remediation:**

4. **Monitor for Updates**: Stay in close contact with the software vendor for updates on the vulnerability and the availability of patches. Also, monitor trusted cybersecurity sources for any developments or additional mitigations.

5. **Testing and Deployment of Patches**: Once a patch is available, prioritize its testing to ensure it does not disrupt business operations. After successful testing, deploy the patch according to your organization's patch management policy, prioritizing the most critical systems.

**Communication Strategy:**

6. **Immediate Notification**: Communicate the presence of the zero-day vulnerability to relevant stakeholders within the

organization, including IT staff, security teams, and management. Explain the potential risks and the immediate steps taken to mitigate them.

7. **Regular Updates**: Provide regular updates to the organization about the status of the vulnerability, including any temporary workarounds implemented, the availability of patches, and the progress of patch deployment.

8. **Instructions for Employees**: If there are actions that employees need to take, such as avoiding the use of certain features or applying updates, provide clear and concise instructions. Make sure to explain the importance of these actions in mitigating the risk.

## Post-Incident Review and Improvement:

9. **Incident Review**: After the vulnerability has been patched and the immediate risk mitigated, conduct a review of the incident. Assess how it was handled, what could have been done better, and the effectiveness of the communication strategy.

10. **Lessons Learned**: Based on the incident review, identify lessons learned and areas for improvement in your organization's cybersecurity practices. This might involve updating incident response plans, improving patch management processes, or enhancing employee training on cybersecurity.

11. **Strengthening Security Posture**: Implement any identified improvements to your security posture to better protect against future vulnerabilities. This may include investing in advanced security tools, enhancing network segmentation, or conducting regular security awareness training.

## 8. DDoS Attack Scenario

**Question**: "Your organization is experiencing a Distributed Denial of Service (DDoS) attack, affecting the availability of your online services. What immediate actions would you take to mitigate the impact of the attack? How would you plan to prevent or reduce the impact of future DDoS attacks?"

Responding to a Distributed Denial of Service (DDoS) attack requires immediate action to mitigate its impact and strategic planning to prevent or minimize future attacks. Here's how to approach both the immediate response and long-term prevention:

**Immediate Mitigation Actions:**

1. **Activate the Incident Response Plan**: Quickly activate your organization's incident response plan specific to DDoS attacks. This plan should include contacting the relevant personnel and assigning roles for the response efforts.
2. **Engage with Your Internet Service Provider (ISP)**: Immediately contact your ISP to inform them of the attack. ISPs can often provide immediate assistance by re-routing traffic, implementing rate-limiting, or providing additional bandwidth to absorb the attack's volume.
3. **Implement Traffic Filtering**: Use traffic filtering solutions to identify and block malicious traffic. This could involve using on-premise or cloud-based DDoS protection services that can detect and mitigate the attack by filtering out attack traffic while allowing legitimate traffic through.
4. **Scale Resources if Possible**: Temporarily scale up bandwidth and server resources if possible, to absorb and disperse the attack's volume. Cloud services can be particularly effective in providing the elasticity needed to respond to the attack's demands.
5. **Apply Rate Limiting**: Implement rate limiting on your routers and firewalls to control the amount of traffic allowed to reach your servers. This can help in preventing your servers from becoming overwhelmed by the attack.
6. **Communicate with Stakeholders**: Keep internal stakeholders and, if necessary, customers informed about the status of the attack and the steps being taken to mitigate its impact. Clear and timely communication can help manage expectations and reduce panic.

**Long-term Prevention and Reduction Strategies:**

7. **Build Redundancy and Resilience**: Design your network architecture for redundancy and resilience. This can involve diversifying your infrastructure across multiple data centers or using cloud services to distribute your services geographically, reducing the risk of a single point of failure.

8. **Establish a Baseline of Normal Traffic**: Understand your normal traffic patterns so you can quickly identify anomalies that may indicate a DDoS attack. Continuous monitoring is key to early detection.

9. **Invest in DDoS Protection Services**: Consider subscribing to specialized DDoS protection services that offer advanced mitigation capabilities beyond what your organization can implement in-house. These services can provide additional layers of defense by analyzing traffic and responding to threats in real-time.

10. **Regularly Update and Test Your Incident Response Plan**: Regularly review and update your incident response plan to reflect new threats and lessons learned from past incidents. Conduct drills and simulations to ensure your team is well-prepared to respond effectively.

11. **Collaborate with Industry Partners**: Join forums or groups that share information about cybersecurity threats, including DDoS attacks. Information sharing can help you stay ahead of emerging threats and learn from the experiences of others.

12. **Educate and Train Your Staff**: Regularly train your staff on the latest cybersecurity threats and defense mechanisms. A well-informed team is your first line of defense against attacks.

## IAM CYBERSECURITY INTERVIEW QUESTIONS

Here are some interview questions related to Identity and Access Management (IAM) in cybersecurity, along with brief answers to give you an idea of what might be expected in such discussions:

### 1. What is Identity and Access Management (IAM), and why is it important?

IAM is a framework of policies and technologies ensuring that the right individuals have access to the technology resources they need at the right times for the right reasons. It's crucial for security and regulatory compliance, helping prevent unauthorized access to sensitive information and resources.

### 2. Can you explain the difference between authentication and authorization?

Authentication is the process of verifying a user's identity, typically through credentials like usernames and passwords, biometrics, or tokens. Authorization occurs after authentication, determining which resources a user can access and what actions they can perform.

### 3. What are some common IAM best practices?

Common IAM best practices include implementing strong password policies, using multi-factor authentication (MFA), least privilege access, regular access reviews, and employing single sign-on (SSO) technologies. Additionally, keeping IAM solutions updated and educating users on security hygiene are important.

### 4. How does Single Sign-On (SSO) work, and what are its benefits?

SSO allows users to log in once and gain access to multiple related systems without being prompted to log in again. Benefits include improved user experience, reduced password fatigue, and decreased risk of phishing due to fewer login prompts.

### 5. Describe multi-factor authentication (MFA). Why is it important?

MFA requires users to provide two or more verification factors to gain access to a resource, such as something they know (password), something they have (security token), or something they are (biometric verification). It significantly increases security by adding an extra layer of protection beyond just passwords.

### 6. Explain the concept of least privilege. Why is it important in IAM?

The principle of least privilege means giving users the minimum levels of access—or permissions—needed to perform their job functions. This minimizes the risk of accidental or deliberate misuse of privileged access, reducing the potential for damage from security breaches.

### 7. What are some challenges in implementing IAM solutions?

Challenges include managing the complexity of integrating IAM solutions with existing systems, balancing security with user convenience, ensuring compliance with various regulatory requirements, handling the scale of user management in large organizations, and keeping up with evolving security threats.

### 8. How do you ensure compliance with data protection regulations through IAM?

Ensuring compliance involves implementing IAM controls that enforce data access policies aligned with legal and regulatory requirements. This includes regular audits, access controls based on roles, encryption of data in transit and at rest, and comprehensive logging of access events.

### 9. What role does IAM play in cloud security?

In cloud security, IAM ensures that only authorized users can access cloud-based resources. This involves managing identities and permissions across various cloud services and infrastructure, protecting data and applications hosted in the cloud from unauthorized access.

### 10. How do you stay current with the latest IAM technologies and best practices?

Staying current can involve subscribing to cybersecurity publications, attending industry conferences and webinars, participating in professional forums and networks, continuous learning through courses and certifications, and experimenting with new technologies in safe test environments.

# PENTESTER CYBERSECURITY INTERVIEW QUESTIONS

## 1. What is penetration testing, and why is it important?

Penetration testing, or pentesting, involves simulating cyber attacks on a computer system, network, or web application to identify security vulnerabilities that could be exploited. It's crucial for uncovering and mitigating potential weaknesses before attackers can exploit them, thereby enhancing an organization's security posture.

## 2. Can you describe the different types of penetration testing?

The main types include black-box testing (testing with no prior knowledge of the system), white-box testing (testing with full knowledge of the system), and gray-box testing (testing with partial knowledge). Each type provides different insights and is chosen based on the testing objectives.

## 3. What methodologies do you follow in your penetration testing process?

Common methodologies include the Open Web Application Security Project (OWASP) for web applications, the Penetration Testing Execution Standard (PTES) for general penetration testing, and the Information System Security Assessment Framework (ISSAF) for a comprehensive security assessment.

## 4. How do you stay undetected during a penetration test?

Techniques include mimicking normal user behavior, using proxy servers to mask the origin of the attacks, leveraging encryption to hide malicious payloads, and timing the attacks to avoid peak usage hours or during known monitoring gaps.

## 5. Describe a tool you commonly use in penetration testing and why.

One commonly used tool is Metasploit, a powerful framework for developing and executing exploit code against a remote target machine. It's favored for its extensive database of exploits, payloads, and its ability to craft custom exploits.

## 6. How do you handle false positives during penetration testing?

Handling false positives involves verifying and retesting the findings, using multiple tools or techniques to confirm the results, and manually reviewing the output to distinguish between true vulnerabilities and false alarms.

## 7. What is the importance of the reporting phase in penetration testing?

The reporting phase is crucial as it provides a detailed overview of the vulnerabilities discovered, the potential impact of these vulnerabilities, and recommendations for mitigation. It helps stakeholders understand the risks and prioritize remediation efforts.

## 8. Can you explain the difference between a vulnerability assessment and penetration testing?

A vulnerability assessment identifies and quantifies security vulnerabilities in a system without exploiting them, focusing on breadth rather than depth. Penetration testing goes deeper by attempting to exploit the vulnerabilities to understand the real-world effectiveness of existing security controls.

## 9. What steps do you take to ensure your testing activities are legal and authorized?

Before conducting a penetration test, I ensure there's a formal agreement or contract that defines the scope of the test, the methods to be used, and explicit permission from the owner of the target system. Additionally, I adhere to ethical guidelines and legal requirements relevant to the testing activities.

## 10. How do you prioritize vulnerabilities found during a

**penetration test?**

Vulnerabilities are prioritized based on their severity, the potential impact on the business, the exploitability of the vulnerability, and the value of the assets at risk. This prioritization helps in allocating resources efficiently to address the most critical vulnerabilities first.

**11. Describe a challenging penetration test you have conducted. What made it challenging, and how did you overcome those challenges?**

This answer would vary depending on personal experience but should detail a specific scenario where the pentester faced technical difficulties, complex systems, or strong security measures. Highlighting the approach taken to overcome these challenges, such as innovative thinking, leveraging less common tools, or working closely with the client to refine the testing scope, demonstrates problem-solving skills and adaptability.

These questions and answers are designed to showcase the candidate's technical expertise, problem-solving abilities, and ethical considerations in the field of penetration testing.

## SOC CYBERSECURITY INTERVIEW QUESTIONS

**1. What is the primary function of a Security Operations Center (SOC)?**

The primary function of a SOC is to monitor, detect, analyze, and respond to cybersecurity incidents using a combination of technology solutions and a strong set of processes. SOCs are responsible for ensuring that potential security threats are correctly identified, analyzed, defended, investigated, and reported.

**2. Can you explain the difference between IDS and IPS?**

An Intrusion Detection System (IDS) monitors network and system traffic for suspicious activity and issues alerts when such activity is detected. An Intrusion Prevention System (IPS), on the other hand, not only detects potentially malicious activity but also takes preemptive action to block or prevent such threats from causing harm.

### 3. How do you prioritize security incidents?

Security incidents are prioritized based on their severity, the potential impact on the organization, and the criticality of the affected assets. Factors such as the vulnerability exploited, the threat actor involved, and the sensitivity of the compromised data also play a crucial role in incident prioritization.

### 4. Describe a cybersecurity framework used in SOC operations.

The NIST Cybersecurity Framework is commonly used in SOC operations. It provides a policy framework of computer security guidance for how private sector organizations in the U.S. can assess and improve their ability to prevent, detect, and respond to cyber attacks. It outlines five core functions: Identify, Protect, Detect, Respond, and Recover.

### 5. What is SIEM, and why is it important in a SOC?

Security Information and Event Management (SIEM) is a solution that aggregates and analyzes activity from many different resources across your IT infrastructure. SIEM is crucial in a SOC for real-time visibility into an organization's security posture, providing advanced analytics to identify threats and vulnerabilities, and facilitating rapid response to identified threats.

### 6. How do you stay updated with the latest cybersecurity threats?

Staying updated with the latest cybersecurity threats involves following reputable cybersecurity news sources, participating in forums and professional networks, attending cybersecurity conferences, and engaging in continuous learning through certifications and training.

### 7. What are some common indicators of compromise (IoCs)?

Common IoCs include unusual outbound network traffic, anomalies in privileged user account activities, spikes in database read volumes, geographical irregularities in access patterns, and files with double extensions. These indicators help in identifying potential security incidents.

### 8. Explain the concept of threat hunting in SOC operations.

Threat hunting is a proactive security search through networks, endpoints, and datasets to detect and isolate advanced threats that evade existing security solutions. In SOC operations, threat hunting involves using manual or machine-assisted techniques to identify malicious activities that have not been detected by automated systems.

### 9. How do you manage stress in a high-pressure environment like a SOC?

Managing stress involves maintaining a clear prioritization of tasks, taking regular breaks to avoid burnout, staying organized, and keeping communication lines open with team members for support. It's also important to have a keen interest in cybersecurity, as passion for the field can make challenging situations more engaging and less stressful.

### 10. What steps would you take if you detected a new malware variant in the network?

Upon detecting a new malware variant, I would first isolate the affected systems to prevent the spread. Then, I would analyze the malware to understand its behavior, impact, and propagation methods. This information would be used to update security measures and signatures in tools to detect and block the malware. Finally, I would document the incident and the response actions taken for future reference and report the findings to relevant stakeholders.

These questions are designed to gauge a candidate's understanding of SOC operations, their technical capabilities, and their approach to the dynamic challenges encountered in cybersecurity defense.

# MALWARE ANALYST INTERVIEW QUESTIONS

### 1. What is malware analysis, and why is it important?

Malware analysis is the process of studying malware to understand its functionality, origin, and potential impact. It's important because it helps in developing effective strategies to protect against malware, identify vulnerabilities, and prevent future attacks.

### 2. Can you describe the difference between static and dynamic malware analysis?

Static analysis involves examining the malware without executing it, focusing on the code structure, strings, and binary level to understand its purpose. Dynamic analysis, on the other hand, involves executing the malware in a controlled environment to observe its behavior, network activity, and interaction with other systems.

### 3. What tools do you use for malware analysis, and why?

Common tools include IDA Pro for disassembling and debugging, Wireshark for network traffic analysis, and Cuckoo Sandbox for automating dynamic malware analysis. These tools provide insights into the malware's operation, aiding in its identification and mitigation.

### 4. How do you ensure safety during malware analysis?

Ensuring safety involves conducting analyses within isolated environments, such as virtual machines, to prevent the malware from affecting real systems. It's also important to keep these environments disconnected from the internet and corporate networks to prevent the spread of the malware.

### 5. What is a malware signature, and how is it used?

A malware signature is a unique string or pattern of bytes that identifies specific malware. Antivirus and intrusion detection systems use these signatures to detect and block malware.

### 6. Explain the concept of a sandbox in malware analysis.

A sandbox is a secure, isolated environment where suspicious code can be executed without risk to the host system. It allows analysts to observe the behavior of the code, including any attempts to connect to external servers, changes to file systems, or registry modifications.

### 7. What steps do you take if you discover a zero-day exploit during your analysis?

Upon discovering a zero-day exploit, I would document its behavior, affected systems, and potential impact. This information would be used to develop detection signatures and mitigation strategies. I would then communicate the findings to relevant stakeholders and collaborate with vendors or security communities to patch the vulnerability.

### 8. How do you keep up with new malware trends and techniques?

Keeping up with new malware trends involves following reputable security blogs and news sources, participating in forums and conferences, engaging in continuous learning through courses and certifications, and exchanging knowledge with peers in the security community.

### 9. Describe a challenging malware analysis case you've worked on.

This answer would vary depending on personal experience but should highlight a specific instance where the analyst encountered complex or sophisticated malware. It should detail the approach taken to analyze the malware, the challenges faced, and how they were overcome, emphasizing analytical skills and perseverance.

### 10. What role do you believe machine learning and AI play in malware analysis?

Machine learning and AI can significantly enhance malware analysis by automating the detection of malware variants and identifying patterns or behaviors that may be indicative of new threats. They can process large volumes of data more efficiently than manual methods, improving the speed and accuracy of malware detection.

These questions aim to probe the technical knowledge, practical skills, and experiences of a candidate in the field of malware analysis, highlighting their approach to tackling malware threats and staying abreast of the evolving cybersecurity landscape.

## CERTIFICATES AND ENCRYPTION QUESTIONS

### 1. Can you explain what a digital certificate is and its role in cybersecurity?

A digital certificate is an electronic document used to prove the ownership of a public key. It includes the public key, identity information, and the digital signature of an entity that has verified the certificate's contents. In cybersecurity, it's crucial for establishing secure connections, ensuring data integrity, and authenticating identities.

### 2. Describe the process of a TLS handshake.

A TLS handshake is a protocol that establishes a secure connection between a client and a server. The process involves the server sending its certificate to the client, the client verifying the certificate with the certificate authority (CA), both parties agreeing on encryption algorithms, and the exchange of encrypted keys to establish a secure session.

### 3. What is the difference between symmetric and asymmetric encryption?

Symmetric encryption uses the same key for both encryption and decryption, making it fast but less secure for certain applications since the key must be shared. Asymmetric encryption uses a pair of keys (public and private) where the public key encrypts data and the private key decrypts it, enhancing security but being slower due to complex mathematical operations.

### 4. How does Public Key Infrastructure (PKI) work?

PKI is a framework for managing digital certificates and public-key encryption. It enables users and devices to securely exchange data over networks and verify the identity of the other party. PKI involves the issuance, renewal, and revocation of digital certificates by trusted certificate authorities (CAs).

### 5. Explain the concept of a Certificate Authority (CA).

A Certificate Authority (CA) is a trusted entity that issues digital certificates. The CA verifies the identity of the certificate requester and signs the certificate with its private key, making it possible for others to verify the authenticity of the certificate with the CA's public key.

### 6. What are some common encryption algorithms, and how do they differ?

Common encryption algorithms include AES (Advanced Encryption Standard) for symmetric encryption, and RSA (Rivest-Shamir-Adleman) for asymmetric encryption. AES is known for its speed and security, making it suitable for encrypting data at rest. RSA is used for secure data transmission, such as in digital signatures and SSL certificates, but it's slower than AES due to its computational complexity.

### 7. How do you manage certificate renewals and expirations to avoid service interruptions?

Managing certificate renewals involves maintaining an inventory of all certificates, monitoring their expiration dates with automated tools, and establishing processes for early renewal. Regular audits and employing centralized management tools can help track and renew certificates before they expire, preventing service disruptions.

## 8. What is a certificate revocation list (CRL)?

A Certificate Revocation List (CRL) is a list of digital certificates that have been revoked before their expiration dates by the issuing CA. CRLs are used to check the revocation status of certificates to ensure they are still valid and have not been compromised.

## 9. How do you ensure the security of encryption keys?

Ensuring the security of encryption keys involves using secure key storage solutions, such as hardware security modules (HSMs), employing key management practices that include rotation, and access controls to limit who can use and see the keys. Regular audits and using encryption for the keys themselves are also critical practices.

## 10. Can you explain what Perfect Forward Secrecy (PFS) is and its importance?

Perfect Forward Secrecy (PFS) is a property of secure communication protocols that ensures a session key derived from a set of long-term public and private keys will not be compromised if one of the long-term keys is compromised in the future. PFS is important because it enhances the security of encrypted data sessions, ensuring that the compromise of one key does not lead to the compromise of past or future sessions.

## CLOUD INTERVIEW QUESTIONS

## 1. What are the main security concerns when moving to the cloud?

The main security concerns include data breaches, loss of data control, insufficient identity and access management, insecure APIs, account hijacking, and the shared responsibility model's complexities. Ensuring compliance and managing multi-cloud environments also pose significant challenges.

### 2. Can you explain the Shared Responsibility Model in cloud computing?

The Shared Responsibility Model outlines that cloud providers are responsible for the security of the cloud infrastructure, while customers are responsible for securing the data and applications they run in the cloud. This division varies slightly among IaaS, PaaS, and SaaS, with more customer responsibility in IaaS and less in SaaS.

### 3. How do you secure data at rest in the cloud?

Securing data at rest involves encryption, access controls, and regularly rotating encryption keys. It's also important to use cloud storage services that offer built-in encryption capabilities and to manage who can access the encryption keys.

### 4. What are some best practices for identity and access management (IAM) in the cloud?

Best practices include implementing the principle of least privilege, enforcing multi-factor authentication (MFA), using role-based access control (RBAC), regularly reviewing and revoking unnecessary permissions, and monitoring IAM activities for unusual access patterns or policy violations.

### 5. Describe a cloud security assessment you have conducted. What were the key steps?

A cloud security assessment might start with defining the scope, including the cloud services and data to be assessed. Then, conducting a thorough review of the cloud environment's configuration, IAM policies, network security settings, and data encryption practices. Key steps include identifying vulnerabilities, assessing the impact of potential risks, and recommending mitigations. Documentation and reporting findings to stakeholders are crucial.

## 6. How do you manage encryption keys in the cloud?

Managing encryption keys in the cloud involves using a key management system (KMS) that allows for the creation, rotation, and deletion of keys securely. Best practices include limiting access to keys, using hardware security modules (HSMs) for high-value keys, and ensuring keys are rotated regularly to reduce the impact of a potential compromise.

## 7. What is CASB, and how does it enhance cloud security?

A Cloud Access Security Broker (CASB) is a security policy enforcement point that sits between cloud service consumers and cloud service providers to enforce security policies as cloud-based resources are accessed. CASB enhances cloud security by providing visibility into cloud application usage, data protection, threat protection, and compliance management across multiple cloud platforms.

## 8. How do you ensure compliance with data protection regulations in the cloud?

Ensuring compliance involves understanding the specific regulatory requirements, selecting cloud providers that offer compliance certifications, implementing data protection measures like encryption and access controls, and conducting regular audits. It's also important to manage data residency by choosing data centers in locations that comply with jurisdictional requirements.

## 9. Explain the importance of network segmentation in the cloud.

Network segmentation in the cloud involves dividing a cloud network into subnetworks to enhance security and reduce the attack surface. It's important for isolating workloads, protecting sensitive data, and containing potential breaches. Segmentation helps in applying targeted security policies and controls to different segments based on their risk levels and requirements.

### 10. How do you approach incident response in a cloud environment?

Incident response in the cloud involves preparing an incident response plan tailored to the cloud environment, including roles and responsibilities, communication protocols, and recovery procedures. It requires integrating cloud-specific tools for monitoring and automation to quickly detect and respond to incidents. Coordination with the cloud provider for access to logs and collaboration during investigations is also critical.

## ENDPOINT AND DEVICE SECURITY QUESTIONS

### 1. What is endpoint security, and why is it important?

Endpoint security refers to the practice of securing end-user devices like desktops, laptops, and mobile devices from malicious threats and vulnerabilities. It's crucial because endpoints are often the target of attacks due to their accessibility and the valuable data they access and store.

### 2. Describe the difference between antivirus and EDR solutions.

Antivirus software focuses on detecting and removing known malware based on signatures, providing a basic level of protection. Endpoint Detection and Response (EDR) solutions offer more advanced capabilities, including continuous monitoring, behavior analysis, and automated response to threats, addressing both known and unknown malware.

### 3. How do you secure mobile devices in a BYOD environment?

Securing mobile devices in a BYOD environment involves

implementing mobile device management (MDM) or mobile application management (MAM) solutions, enforcing strong authentication and encryption, applying regular software updates, and educating users about security best practices.

## 4. What strategies can be used to protect against zero-day exploits?

Strategies include keeping software up to date to reduce vulnerabilities, using intrusion detection systems to monitor unusual activity, implementing least privilege access, employing sandboxing to isolate applications, and utilizing threat intelligence to stay informed about emerging threats.

## 5. How does patch management contribute to endpoint security?

Patch management is vital for correcting security vulnerabilities and software bugs in operating systems and applications. By regularly applying patches, organizations can protect endpoints from being exploited by attackers using known vulnerabilities.

## 6. Can you explain what a VPN is and how it contributes to device security?

A Virtual Private Network (VPN) creates a secure, encrypted connection over a less secure network, such as the internet. It helps protect data transmission, ensures anonymity, and secures remote access, contributing to the overall security of devices by preventing eavesdropping and man-in-the-middle attacks.

## 7. What considerations should be taken into account when implementing disk encryption?

When implementing disk encryption, consider the encryption method (hardware vs. software-based), the strength of encryption algorithms, key management practices, the impact on system performance, and compliance with regulatory requirements.

## 8. Describe how you would respond to a ransomware attack on several endpoints.

Responding to a ransomware attack involves isolating the affected endpoints to prevent the spread of malware, identifying the ransomware variant, using backups to restore encrypted files, and removing the ransomware from infected devices. It's also important to analyze the attack vector and improve defenses to prevent future incidents.

## 9. How do you ensure compliance with data protection regulations at the endpoint level?

Ensuring compliance involves implementing data encryption, access controls, and audit trails on endpoints. Regularly reviewing and updating security policies and endpoint configurations to align with regulatory requirements is also crucial.

## 10. What is the role of user training in endpoint security?

User training is fundamental to endpoint security as it educates users on recognizing and avoiding security threats like phishing, malware, and unsafe online practices. Informed users are less likely to inadvertently compromise their devices and the network.

ABOUT THE AUTHOR

Maria Bryght is a seasoned IT consultant, educator, and author with over two decades of experience in the technology industry. Maria has dedicated her career to advancing IT practices, cybersecurity, and Identity and Access Management (IAM) strategies across various sectors. Her contributions to the field are also captured in her writing. She is the author of several influential books on cybersecurity and IT in general, recognized for their clarity, depth, and practical guidance.

www.ingramcontent.com/pod-product-compliance
Lightning Source LLC
Chambersburg PA
CBHW071135050326
40690CB00008B/1472